JAMES A. GAZELL

# The FUTURE of
# STATE COURT MANAGEMENT

National University Publications
KENNIKAT PRESS    //    1978
Port Washington, N. Y.    //    London

Manufactured in the United States of America

Published by
**Kennikat Press Corp.**
Port Washington, N. Y. / London

**Library of Congress Cataloging in Publication Data**

Gazell, James A
    The future of state court management.

    (Kennikat Press multi-disciplinary studies in
the law) (National university publications)
    Includes bibliographical references and indexes.
    1. Court administration—United States—States.
    2. Courts—United States—States. I. Title.
KF8732.Z95G39      347'.73'3          77-22996
ISBN 0-8046-9195-9

# THE FUTURE OF
# STATE COURT MANAGEMENT

Kennikat Press

**National University Publications**

Multi-disciplinary Studies in the Law

*General Editor*

Rudolph J. Gerber
*Arizona State University*

*To Monica: My Loving Bride*

# ACKNOWLEDGEMENTS

This study is primarily an adaptation of five articles recently completed by the author. The first section is drawn from "Lower Court Unification in the American States," which appeared in the *Arizona State Law Journal,* (Fall 1974) 653-87; the second section from "State Judicial Financing: Preliminaries, Progress, Provisions, and Prognosis," which was published in the *Kentucky Law Journal* 63, no. 1 (1974-75): 73-105; the third section from "A Taxonomy of State Court Personnel Management," which appeared in the *St. John's Law Review* 46 (Fall 1974): 74-96; and the fourth section from "Judicial Reorganization in Michigan," which was published in the *Michigan State Bar Journal* 54 (February 1975): 113-21, and "Probation and State-Court Reform: The Location Issue" (written with Edward S. Piggins, Jr.), which has not yet been published. Permission to adapt these essays for use in this book was obtained from each of these journals.

# CONTENTS

# THE FUTURE OF
# STATE COURT MANAGEMENT

# FOREWORD

> *Court administration—the management of the non-*
> *judicial business of a court or court system—clearly is a*
> *matter of high priority in any reexamination of court*
> *processing of criminal defendants . . .*
> *The Commission is convinced that efficient judicial*
> *administration requires the creation of a centralized court*
> *administration within each jurisdiction.* [1]

This comment, made recently by the National Advisory Commission on Criminal Justice Standards and Goals, is merely the latest indication that the field of federal and state court management has been assuming greater importance. With mounting public concern over increasing crime rates and court congestion, the subject will probably become even more salient.

This study examines some current and prospective directions of court management, especially at the state level. Its central theme is that the area of court management is moving steadily toward the attainment of three overlapping objectives—the unification of state judiciaries, the statewide financing of all courts, and the emergence of state court personnel systems —and that progress toward these goals converges to bring such institutions closer to the ideal of judicial systems that are honest, competent, equitable, and effective.

The art of judicial administration presumes that significant advances toward such a utopia depend, in part, on structural and operational changes in the court segments of the judicial system. Such alterations will enable these organizations to cope with their business more rapidly and fairly. Conventional thought in this field assumes that internal changes, especially in procedures, techniques, and the greater use of technology, will be the most instrumental paths toward raising the quality of judicial performance. Nonetheless, it is acknowledged that refurbishment of court machinery itself may not suffice and that it may become necessary to restrict the scope of the judicial business. Specifically, it is realized that some criminal and civil inputs into court bureaucracies may have to be reduced. Substantial improvement in court management may necessitate far-reaching changes in the external milieu. States may have to control the flow of cases by eliminating what are sometimes called victimless crimes: abortions, drunkenness, gambling, juvenile offenses, minor drug abuse, sexual conduct between consenting adults, vagrancy, and disorderly conduct. Moreover, states may need to lessen the influx of civil litigation by passing no-fault automobile insurance statutes and removing probate cases from the courts.[2] However, it is axiomatic in judicial management that courts themselves still bear the cardinal responsibility for their own performance and should not depend too much on such reductions in caseloads. Although it is generally recognized that improved judicial operations also presume extensive cooperation from police and correctional agencies (the other principal sectors of the justice system), the courts' primary responsibility continues unchanged.

Therefore, this study centers on what courts *per se* have proposed or done to alter their internal environments and to upgrade their effectiveness. The four sections of this book examine recent progress along a specific dimension toward an ideal judicial system. The first section reviews the subject of court unification with: a prelude, the evolution of the unification idea, its advocacy, its measurement, patterns of unification before 1970, current progress, and a forecast. The second section delves into the matter of state court financing: the meaning and significance of this concept, the momentum of changes in court financing, the main categories of such changes, and a prognosis. The third section examines the subject of court personnel: it includes judges, court-related employees, appropriate models, and the probable future. The fourth section centers upon some ancillary developments.

My research made use of historical, legalistic, and empirical methods. Data was culled from a variety of sources, including the American Judicature Society, the Bethune-Jones Corporation, the Institute of Judicial Administration, and the court administrator's office in thirty-seven of the fifty states. The information embraces a time span from 1906 to August, 1976, and may prove helpful to judges, court administrators, legal scholars, practicing attorneys, political scientists, and sociologists. The impetus for this study came from my work as a technical advisor for the nationally respected consulting firm of Ernst and Ernst, which had received a grant from the Law Enforcement Assistance Administration to investigate the Michigan court system. The general managers of this firm—Eugene W. Kuthy and Charles W. Barkdull—provided invaluable guidance. Joseph and Elsie Ellenbogen and Melissa Pitkin deserve much gratitude for their outstanding typing work.

# 1

# PROGRESS IN
# STATE COURT UNIFICATION

*Unification of the courts [of limited or special original jurisdiction] would go far to enable the judiciary to do adequately much which in desperation of efficient legal disposition by fettered courts, tied to cumbersome and technical procedure, we have been committing more and more to administrative boards and commissions. Ours is historically a legal polity and the balance of our institutions will be sadly disturbed if the courts lose their place in it. If they are to keep that place they must be organized to compete effectively with the newer administrative bodies.*[1]

This comment, made in 1940 by the eminent legal scholar Roscoe Pound, is merely one illustration of the salience that the subject of lower-court unification achieved during the first half of the twentieth century. For scholars in judicial administration and numerous court officials, this aim became a Holy Grail, a supreme object of quest by the knights of the judicial realm. Like the Grail, the consolidation of tribunals with limited or special original jurisdiction in every state is almost universally regarded as both an instrument of court regeneration and the path of judicial grace —court systems that are competent, effective, uniform, and equitable. Before the end of this century this judicial Grail may be captured as all the states share in its putative blessings.

As the foremost aspect of judicial administration at the state level, specialists have paid increasing attention to this subject. Interest began with Pound in 1906, who popularized the judicial unification system installed by the British in 1875.[2] Despite Pound's repeated advocacy,[3] lower-court unification continued to be generally ignored inside as well as outside of the legal profession until after World War II when a few states gave serious consideration to this matter. Since 1960, the interest of the states in this facet of court management has mushroomed. That attention has expressed itself in three forms: changes in the state judicial articles; enactment of court legislation or judicial article revisions; and examination of numerous state judicial structures. A survey of developments affecting court unification in the fifty states requires an exploration of the following six areas: (1) an evolutionary perspective toward minor court unification; (2) kinds of unification that have been widely advocated; (3) measurement of lower-court unification; (4) patterns of such mergers (1936-70); (5) the latest data pertinent to such models (1971-73); and (6) a prognosis.

## THE EVOLUTION OF THE UNIFICATION CONCEPT

A valid exploration of the lower-court unification movement within judicial administration presumes widespread agreement on the meaning of unification, which so far has been used to denote two ideas. First, unification signifies administrative direction by the supreme court over the entire state judicial system. Such managerial supervision is generally thought to embrace at least four components.

1. It entails the passage of laws authorizing the highest court in the state to make all rules of practice and procedure with or without the retention of a legislative veto power.[4] The state supreme court may delegate this power to its chief justice, to an administrative office of the courts, or to both.

2. Such direction has increasingly denoted the right of one of these three sources to appoint the managerial personnel for the rest of the court system—especially the chief judges and judicial administrators at the appellate- and trial-court levels. These appointees serve at the pleasure of the chief justice, the supreme court, or the administrative director. Since 1966, Colorado, the model for centralized appointive power, has allowed its chief justice to select not only the state court administrator and deputies but also the chief judges of the trial courts and the trial-court administrators and assistants.[5] Pennsylvania in 1968 and Iowa in 1971 are states that have adopted the Colorado paradigm.[6]

However, this schema has recently come under attack from two sources (the Institute for Court Management in Denver[7] and the American Judicature Society[8]) for a number of reasons, including doubts about the feasibility of the model, skepticism about its desirability even if feasible, faith in state judicial councils as the best policy-making organs, a belief in decentralization, a fear of misdirection from the top, the remoteness of top management, a view of widespread judicial participation in policy formation as a requirement for genuine support and substantial compliance, and a failure to recognize the complexity of the court system and the ability of its segments to thwart managerial initiatives from the top. Instead, a collegial model, with the trial judges appointing their chief, who in turn, will choose the local court administrators and deputies, has been recommended.

3. Managerial supervision includes the right of the highest state court or its agents to assign all court personnel at will. The right of assignment consists of numerous aspects. It applies not only to judges but also to all court-related personnel. It extends to all tiers of the state court system It encompasses the vertical and horizontal transfer of judges and court executives on a temporary basis, usually no longer than a year. It extends this power to retired judges, who may consent to serve at any court level in the state.

4. Such oversight embraces statewide judicial financing through a yearly budget prepared by the highest state court (or its administrator) and submitted to the state legislature for its consideration. This financing is generally regarded as a *sine qua non* and as a complement of rule-making, appointive, and assigning controls. At present a dozen states have taken this step.

Second, the unification idea signifies that administrative direction over an entire state court system may be divided not only by function but also by level—appellate and trial and court. At the appellate level, unification has entailed combining the functions of a civil appeals court and a criminal appeals court into one intermediate court of appeals. Three states (Georgia, Kentucky, and Texas) have considered this mode of unification.[9]

At the trial-court level, five patterns, which will be detailed later, are evident:

1. Some states have tended to make piecemeal changes, such as consolidating all courts in certain counties or cities.

2. Other states are inclined to establish or retain one trial court of general

original jurisdiction while reducing the number of levels of trial courts with limited or special criminal and civil jurisdiction (often called minor or lower courts). These minor courts exist at the state, county, and municipal and township levels. Reductions are obtained either by abolishing justice-of-the-peace courts and other fee offices or by drastically curtailing their criminal and civil jurisdictions.

3. Some jurisdictions have set up one statewide general trial court while creating a single tier of lower courts to operate throughout the state. The result of such changes is a two-tier trial-court system rather than the multilayer (three or more) trial-court apparatus characteristic of the first pattern. Both approaches represent incremental attempts at unification, albeit to different extents.

4. Several states have put into operation a single trial court of general jurisdiction while abolishing all minor court tiers. In 1962, Illinois became the first state to traverse this route when its new judicial article provided for a system of circuit courts as the only kind of trial court.[10]

5. Numerous states are studying the possible ways by which trial courts may be unified in one form or another.

## THE ADVOCACY OF UNIFICATION

The advocacy of lower-court unification in the states has demonstrated consensus and fragmentation. One finds widespread agreement that consolidation embraces centralized rule-making, appointive, assigning, and budgetary functions as well as a single intermediate appellate court in each state. However, no consensus exists about the best pattern of such unification beyond the necessity of eliminating fee offices and transferring their functions to courts of record and the advisability of phasing in basic or incremental judicial changes over a period of two or more years.

Two outlooks predominate. One may be called the Pound ideal of one state court of justice, with a judicial council as a policy-making body (composed of judges, lawyers, and laymen), state and local court administrators, one final appellate court (a supreme court), a general trial court (superior court) with appellate divisions, and a county court with limited original jurisdiction. In 1906, Pound urged this model (without including the last set of courts) in what has been almost universally regarded as a landmark address before the American Bar Association. Although Pound later added a layer of county courts, espousal of the original model has been continued by such eminent judicial administration scholars as Glenn Winters, the Executive Director of the American Judicature Society.[11] As previously mentioned, Illinois has most nearly approximated this ideal. The advantages of this model are many: its simplicity through the elimination of all unnecessary trial courts; its eradication of concurrent jurisdiction; its conservation of judicial power; and its flexibility, especially from budgetary and assignment standpoints. Moreover, this schema assumes that the condition of the lower courts is irremediable; that they will always be a stepchild of state judicial systems if retained; that there is no means of transforming them into competent, impartial, and effective tribunals; and that euthanasia is preferable to keeping them alive with bandages and aspirin. However, the main drawback to this model is its political unfeasibility. Among the common reasons for opposition are fears of judicial centralization, the costs of attaining this goal, and the vested interests of a variety of trial judges who do not want any curtailment of their broad powers.

Pound's revised model has garnered the most attention among court-management experts. With the growing workloads of state judicial systems, exponents of the revised model have urged the establishment of an intermediate court of appeals. Among the most notable proponents of this approach have been the National Commission on Law Observance and Enforcement (generally known as the Wickersham Commission) in 1931.[12] the American Bar Association (1962),[13] the American Judicature Society (1962),[14] the National Municipal League (1963),[15] the President's Commission on Law Enforcement and the Administration of Justice (1967),[16] the National Advisory Commission on Civil Disorders (1968),[17] the National Conference on the Judiciary at Williamsburg, Virginia (1971),[18] the Advisory Commission on Intergovernmental Relations (1971),[19] the Committee on Economic Development (1972),[20] and the National Commission on Criminal Justice Standards and Goals (1973).[21] This pattern is the one toward which states are generally edging. The popularity of the revised model stems largely from its political feasibility and belated recognition of lower-court salience, since these tribunals are usually the only ones that the public encounters and since more than 90 percent of all criminal and civil cases start and end in these courts. The main disadvantage of this model is that it is not nearly as centralized as the original model.

## THE MEASUREMENT OF LOWER-COURT UNIFICATION

A review of definitional and hortatory aspects of lower-court unification leads to an examination of measurements for the achievement of this goal. No generally accepted criteria exist for making such a quantitative analysis. In fact, the literature in judicial administration ignores this subject. However, such measurement is inherently a segment of two larger rubrics: state court unification in general and judicial modernization. (See Figs. 1-1 and 1-2.)

As Figure 1-1 makes clear, it is possible to measure lower-court consolidation as part of a device that encompasses one of the following seven standards.

1. The presence of a court administrator's office: (4 points = presence; 0 points = absence).

2. The authority of the state supreme court or its administrative office to make rules of civil and criminal procedure and practice for the entire judicial system: (4 points = presence of both; 2 points = presence of either civil or criminal; 0 points = absence of both).

3. The scope of a state supreme court's assignment power, including the lower courts: (A total of 4 points. 1 point = upward; 1 point = downward; 1 point = horizontal; 1 point = assignment of retired judges).

4. The enactment of state court financing—90 to 100 percent of all judicial costs: (4 points = presence; 2 points = 40-90 percent state share; 0 points = under 40 percent state share).

5. The presence of one intermediate court of appeals: 94 points = 1 type; 2 points = 2 types or more; 0 points = no such court).

6. The kinds of general trial courts: (4 points = 1 kind; 2 points = 2 kinds; 0 points = 3 or more kinds).

Sources: Derived from: "Listing of Courts of Limited and Special Jurisdiction, by Level of Organization, by State," "Table 1, Number of Courts by Level of Jurisdiction, by Region and State," and an untitled, updated list of highest state courts, intermediate appellate courts, general trial courts, and court administrators furnished by Richard F. Buckley, Research Assistant for the American Judicature Society, 1155 East 60th Street, Chicago, Illinois 60637, with a letter dated October 17, 1973. Buckley updated the first list from September, 1972, to October, 1973. See also "State Court Progress at a Glance," *Judicature* 56 (May 1973): 427-30; Henry R. Glick and Kenneth N. Vines, *State Court Systems* (Englewood Cliffs, N.J.: Prentice-Hall, 1973), pp. 28-30; Advisory Commission on Intergovernmental Relations, A Commission Report, *State-Local Relations in the Criminal Justice System* (Washington, D.C.: U.S. Government Printing Office, 1971), pp. 108, 192, 206-7; *State and Local Court Financing (A Tentative Report)* (New York: The Institute of Judicial Administration, Inc., 1969), pp. 27-28, 30-31; and the *California Lower Court Study* (San Francisco: Booz, Allen and Hamilton, Inc., 1971), Appendix F, p. 2; *California Unified Trial Court Feasibility Study* (San Francisco: Booz, Allen and Hamilton, Inc., 1971), p. 45; "Georgia Gets Its First Court Administrative Office," *Judicature* 8 (March 1974): 372.

## Figure 1-1: Measurements of Court Unification in the States (1975)

| States | Court Admin. Office | Rule Making Power | Assignment Power | State Court Financing | Intermed. Appellate Courts | Kinds of General Trial Courts | Kinds of Lower Courts | Total Points |
|---|---|---|---|---|---|---|---|---|
| 1. Alabama | 4 | 4 | 0 | 0 | 2 | 4 | 2 | 16 |
| 2. Alaska | 4 | 4 | 4 | 4 | 0 | 4 | 3 | 23 |
| 3. Arizona | 4 | 4 | 4 | 0 | 4 | 4 | 2 | 22 |
| 4. Arkansas | 4 | 4 | 2 | 0 | 0 | 2 | 0 | 12 |
| 5. California | 4 | 4 | 0 | 0 | 4 | 4 | 2 | 18 |
| 6. Colorado | 4 | 4 | 4 | 4 | 4 | 4 | 0 | 24 |
| 7. Connecticut | 4 | 2 | 4 | 4 | 0 | 4 | 0 | 18 |
| 8. Delaware | 4 | 4 | 2 | 0 | 0 | 2 | 0 | 12 |
| 9. Florida | 4 | 4 | 0 | 4 | 4 | 2 | 0 | 18 |
| 10. Georgia | 4 | 2 | 0 | 0 | 4 | 2 | 0 | 12 |
| 11. Hawaii | 4 | 4 | 4 | 4 | 0 | 4 | 3 | 23 |
| 12. Idaho | 4 | 4 | 4 | 0 | 0 | 4 | 4 | 20 |
| 13. Illinois | 4 | 4 | 4 | 0 | 4 | 4 | 4 | 24 |
| 14. Indiana | 4 | 2 | 0 | 0 | 4 | 2 | 0 | 12 |
| 15. Iowa | 4 | 4 | 0 | 0 | 0 | 4 | 4 | 16 |
| 16. Kansas | 4 | 4 | 0 | 0 | 0 | 4 | 4 | 16 |
| 17. Kentucky | 4 | 4 | 4 | 4 | 4 | 4 | 4 | 28 |
| 18. Louisiana | 4 | 4 | 0 | 0 | 4 | 4 | 0 | 16 |
| 19. Maine | 4 | 4 | 0 | 4 | 0 | 4 | 2 | 18 |
| 20. Maryland | 4 | 4 | 0 | 4 | 4 | 4 | 2 | 22 |
| 21. Massachusetts | 4 | 4 | 0 | 0 | 0 | 4 | 0 | 12 |
| 22. Michigan | 4 | 4 | 0 | 0 | 4 | 4 | 0 | 16 |
| 23. Minnesota | 4 | 2 | 0 | 0 | 0 | 4 | 0 | 10 |
| 24. Mississippi | 0 | 0 | 0 | 0 | 0 | 2 | 0 | 2 |
| 25. Missouri | 4 | 4 | 0 | 0 | 4 | 4 | 0 | 16 |
| 26. Montana | 0 | 4 | 0 | 0 | 0 | 4 | 0 | 8 |
| 27. Nebraska | 4 | 4 | 2 | 0 | 0 | 4 | 0 | 14 |
| 28. Nevada | 4 | 4 | 0 | 0 | 0 | 4 | 0 | 12 |
| 29. New Hampshire | 0 | 4 | 2 | 0 | 0 | 4 | 1 | 11 |
| 30. New Jersey | 4 | 4 | 0 | 0 | 4 | 4 | 0 | 16 |
| 31. New Mexico | 4 | 4 | 0 | 4 | 4 | 4 | 0 | 20 |
| 32. New York | 4 | 4 | 4 | 0 | 4 | 4 | 0 | 20 |
| 33. North Carolina | 4 | 2 | 4 | 4 | 4 | 4 | 3 | 25 |
| 34. North Dakota | 4 | 2 | 4 | 0 | 0 | 4 | 4 | 18 |
| 35. Ohio | 4 | 2 | 4 | 0 | 4 | 4 | 0 | 18 |
| 36. Oklahoma | 4 | 0 | 4 | 4 | 4 | 4 | 0 | 20 |
| 37. Oregon | 4 | 0 | 0 | 0 | 4 | 4 | 0 | 12 |
| 38. Pennsylvania | 4 | 4 | 4 | 0 | 4 | 4 | 0 | 20 |
| 39. Rhode Island | 4 | 4 | 0 | 4 | 0 | 4 | 0 | 16 |
| 40. South Carolina | 4 | 4 | 0 | 0 | 0 | 4 | 4 | 16 |
| 41. South Dakota | 4 | 4 | 0 | 0 | 0 | 4 | 4 | 16 |
| 42. Tennessee | 4 | 2 | 0 | 0 | 2 | 0 | 0 | 8 |
| 43. Texas | 0 | 2 | 0 | 0 | 2 | 4 | 0 | 8 |
| 44. Utah | 4 | 4 | 2 | 0 | 0 | 4 | 0 | 14 |
| 45. Vermont | 4 | 2 | 4 | 4 | 0 | 4 | 1 | 19 |
| 46. Virginia | 4 | 4 | 2 | 0 | 0 | 0 | 0 | 10 |
| 47. Washington | 4 | 2 | 0 | 0 | 4 | 4 | 0 | 14 |
| 48. West Virginia | 4 | 2 | 2 | 0 | 0 | 4 | 0 | 12 |
| 49. Wisconsin | 4 | 2 | 4 | 0 | 0 | 4 | 3 | 17 |
| 50. Wyoming | 0 | 4 | 0 | 0 | 0 | 4 | 4 | 12 |
| Total states with perfect scores | 45 | 34 | 16 | 13 | 24 | 42 | 9 | (range 2–28) |

## Figure 1-2: Additional Indexes of State Court Modernization (1973)

| States | Merit Plan | Mandatory Service | Service after Retirement | Unified Bar | Judicial Compensation Commissions | Judicial Qualification Com. | A.B.A. Code of Judicial Conduct | Modernization Total Points | Unification and Modernization Total |
|---|---|---|---|---|---|---|---|---|---|
| 1. Alabama | 0 | 4 | 4 | 4 | 0 | 4 | 4 | 20 | 36 |
| 2. Alaska | 4 | 4 | 4 | 4 | 0 | 4 | 0 | 20 | 43 |
| 3. Arizona | 0 | 0 | 4 | 4 | 4 | 0 | 0 | 12 | 34 |
| 4. Arkansas | 0 | 0 | 4 | 0 | 0 | 4 | 0 | 8 | 20 |
| 5. California | 0 | 0 | 4 | 4 | 0 | 4 | 0 | 12 | 30 |
| 6. Colorado | 4 | 4 | 4 | 0 | 0 | 4 | 0 | 16 | 40 |
| 7. Connecticut | 0 | 4 | 4 | 0 | 4 | 4 | 4 | 20 | 38 |
| 8. Delaware | 0 | 0 | 0 | 0 | 0 | 0 | 0 | 0 | 12 |
| 9. Florida | 4 | 4 | 4 | 4 | 4 | 4 | 4 | 28 | 46 |
| 10. Georgia | 0 | 4 | 4 | 4 | 4 | 4 | 0 | 20 | 32 |
| 11. Hawaii | 0 | 4 | 4 | 0 | 0 | 4 | 0 | 12 | 35 |
| 12. Idaho | 4 | 4 | 4 | 4 | 0 | 4 | 0 | 20 | 40 |
| 13. Illinois | 0 | 4 | 4 | 0 | 4 | 4 | 0 | 16 | 40 |
| 14. Indiana | 4 | 4 | 0 | 0 | 0 | 4 | 0 | 12 | 24 |
| 15. Iowa | 4 | 2 | 4 | 0 | 4 | 4 | 0 | 18 | 34 |
| 16. Kansas | 4 | 4 | 4 | 0 | 0 | 4 | 0 | 16 | 32 |
| 17. Kentucky | 0 | 0 | 0 | 4 | 0 | 0 | 0 | 4 | 32 |
| 18. Louisiana | 4 | 4 | 4 | 4 | 0 | 4 | 0 | 20 | 36 |
| 19. Maine | 0 | 0 | 4 | 0 | 0 | 0 | 0 | 4 | 22 |
| 20. Maryland | 0 | 4 | 0 | 0 | 0 | 4 | 0 | 8 | 30 |
| 21. Massachusetts | 0 | 4 | 0 | 0 | 0 | 0 | 4 | 8 | 20 |
| 22. Michigan | 0 | 4 | 4 | 4 | 4 | 4 | 0 | 20 | 36 |
| 23. Minnesota | 0 | 2 | 4 | 0 | 4 | 4 | 0 | 14 | 24 |
| 24. Mississippi | 0 | 0 | 0 | 4 | 0 | 0 | 0 | 4 | 6 |
| 25. Missouri | 4 | 4 | 4 | 4 | 0 | 4 | 0 | 20 | 36 |
| 26. Montana | 0 | 4 | 4 | 0 | 4 | 4 | 0 | 16 | 24 |
| 27. Nebraska | 4 | 4 | 0 | 4 | 0 | 4 | 0 | 16 | 30 |
| 28. Nevada | 0 | 0 | 0 | 4 | 0 | 0 | 0 | 4 | 16 |
| 29. New Hampshire | 0 | 4 | 4 | 4 | 0 | 0 | 4 | 16 | 27 |
| 30. New Jersey | 0 | 4 | 4 | 0 | 0 | 0 | 0 | 8 | 24 |
| 31. New Mexico | 0 | 0 | 0 | 4 | 0 | 4 | 0 | 8 | 28 |
| 32. New York | 0 | 4 | 4 | 0 | 4 | 4 | 4 | 20 | 40 |
| 33. North Carolina | 0 | 2 | 4 | 4 | 0 | 4 | 0 | 14 | 39 |
| 34. North Dakota | 0 | 0 | 4 | 4 | 0 | 0 | 0 | 8 | 26 |
| 35. Ohio | 0 | 4 | 4 | 0 | 4 | 4 | 0 | 16 | 34 |
| 36. Oklahoma | 4 | 0 | 4 | 4 | 0 | 4 | 0 | 16 | 36 |
| 37. Oregon | 0 | 4 | 4 | 4 | 0 | 4 | 0 | 16 | 28 |
| 38. Pennsylvania | 0 | 4 | 4 | 0 | 4 | 0 | 0 | 12 | 32 |
| 39. Rhode Island | 0 | 0 | 4 | 0 | 0 | 4 | 0 | 8 | 24 |
| 40. South Carolina | 0 | 4 | 4 | 4 | 0 | 4 | 0 | 16 | 32 |
| 41. South Dakota | 0 | 4 | 4 | 4 | 4 | 4 | 0 | 20 | 36 |
| 42. Tennessee | 4 | 0 | 4 | 0 | 0 | 4 | 0 | 12 | 20 |
| 43. Texas | 0 | 4 | 4 | 4 | 0 | 4 | 0 | 16 | 24 |
| 44. Utah | 4 | 2 | 4 | 4 | 4 | 4 | 0 | 22 | 36 |
| 45. Vermont | 4 | 0 | 0 | 0 | 0 | 4 | 0 | 8 | 27 |
| 46. Virginia | 0 | 4 | 4 | 4 | 0 | 4 | 4 | 20 | 30 |
| 47. Washington | 0 | 4 | 4 | 4 | 4 | 0 | 0 | 16 | 30 |
| 48. West Virginia | 0 | 0 | 4 | 4 | 0 | 0 | 4 | 12 | 24 |
| 49. Wisconsin | 0 | 4 | 4 | 4 | 0 | 4 | 0 | 16 | 33 |
| 50. Wyoming | 4 | 4 | 4 | 4 | 0 | 4 | 0 | 20 | 32 |
| Total states with perfect scores | 15 | 31 | 40 | 29 | 15 | 37 | 8 | (range 0–28) | (range 6–46) |

7. The kinds of courts with limited or special jurisdiction: (4 points = none; 3 points = 1 kind; 2 points = 2 kinds; 1 point = 3 kinds; 0 points = 4 kinds or more).

Such criteria for determining and comparing the degree of state court unification are also components of a closely related subject: court modernization, a synthesis of the preceding attributes and at least seven more: the existence of a "merit" (or Missouri) plan of judicial selection at the appellate- and trial-court levels; the existence of a mandatory retirement age for all judicial and court-related personnel; a unified bar with membership as a prerequisite for judicial eligibility; the existence of judicial-qualifications commissions; the presence of judicial-compensation commissions; the use of modern rules of criminal and civil procedure; and the adoption of the American Bar Association code of judicial conduct. (See Fig. 1-2.) Finally the measurement of the variables in figures 1-1 and 1-2 rests on two assumptions. One is that the variables are equally valuable and should be accorded the same weight range (0-4). The other is that this numerical span is large enough to embrace all notable shadings in the extent of compliance with each standard.

Figure 1-1 supplies a quantitative view of the extent to which the states have moved toward the attainment of court unification as measured by the first seven characteristics. Let us briefly consider what this chart discloses with regard to these standards.

1. Forty-five states have an administrative office of the courts.

2. In thirty-four states the supreme court is authorized to make rules of civil and criminal procedure and practice either by itself or subject to a legislative veto.

3. In sixteen states the highest court is empowered to assign lower-court judges as well as all other judges, regardless of level.

4. State-court financing has been adopted in thirteen states.

5. Twenty-four states have set up intermediate courts of appeal.

6. Forty-two states have only one type of general court.

7. Only nine states have abolished their lower courts, although four states have come close and have retained one kind of court in this category.

All told, thirty-one states have proceeded more than halfway (15 to 28 points) toward state court unification. Three states have reached the midpoint (14 points). Sixteen states have not yet reached the halfway mark (0 to 13 points). Three assumptions are implicit in this examination.

---

*Four points = presence or adoption of reform at top of column; 2 points = partial adoption; 0 points = absence.
Sources: See note to Figure 1-1.

One is that court unification represents a continuum along which the various states occupy positions. A second assumption is that these seven criteria indeed measure what they purport to measure. A third assumption is that all of these standards merit equal weight.

## PATTERNS OF UNIFICATION PROGRESS BEFORE 1971

Five patterns of development in lower-court unification are apparent in the states. These have been made since the end of World War II.

### LOWER-COURT CHANGES SHORT OF UNIFICATION

Between 1936 and 1970, at least fourteen states made structural and administrative changes in their lower courts short of unification.

*Virginia (1936, 1956):* Two legislative changes are noteworthy. First, salaried trial judges replaced justices of the peace in various counties. Second, such justices were made municipal or county judges.

*Missouri (1945):* The justice-of-the-peace office was abolished and replaced by salaried magistrates. Further steps toward partial court unification in this state were taken in 1976.

*California (1950):* A spate of minor courts were superseded by two kinds of lower tribunals—municipal courts and their rural counterparts, justice courts.

*Louisiana (1956):* Justice-of-the-peace courts were eliminated and replaced by city judges.

*Minnesota (1956, 1963):* A few changes require mention. First, references to justices of the peace were eliminated from the state constitution, although the office was still retained by statute. Second, in Hennepin County (embracing Minneapolis), this office was abolished. Its functions were absorbed by a unified municipal court.

*New Hampshire (1957, 1963):* The civil and criminal jurisdiction of justices of the peace in this state was removed by legislation. Later, numerous municipal courts were abolished as the remaining thirty-seven became district courts (general trial courts).

*Tennessee (1959):* Courts of General Session were created in all but six counties to replace justices of the peace, who retained nonjudicial functions such as performing marriages.

*Maine (1961):* Justice-of-the-peace and municipal courts were replaced by a single type of lower court—the district court.

*Washington (1961):* In three counties (King, Pierre, and Spokane) justices of the peace and other minor courts were replaced with county-justice courts.

*Delaware (1964):* The justices of the peace in this state were placed under the supervision of the deputy administrator to the state supreme court.

*Oregon (1965):* The office of justice of the peace was abolished in Multnomah County and was replaced by a district court (a general trial court).

*Wyoming (1966):* References to the justice-of-the-peace office were stricken from the state constitution, although these positions remained by statute.

*Maryland (1970):* Justices-of-the-peace and magistrate courts were eliminated and superseded by one statewide lower court: the district court. In late 1972, Governor Marvin Mandel, by executive order, created a commission on judicial reform to study further court unification in this state. Its report was due for completion in 1974.

*Nebraska (1970):* Mention of the justice-of-the-peace office was removed from the state constitution and left this position with only a statutory basis for its continuance.[22]

## PARTIAL UNIFICATION OF THE LOWER COURTS IN THE STATES: TWO OR MORE TIERS PRESERVED

Some states have partially unified their lower courts while retaining two or more tiers with fewer tribunals. The following seventeen states have taken this route,[23] as indicated in figure 1–3.

**Figure 1–3: The Extent of Pattern Two Adoptions**

| State | Year | State | Year |
|-------|------|-------|------|
| New Jersey | 1947 | Delaware | 1965 |
| California | 1950 | Vermont | 1965 |
| Alaska | 1956 | South Dakota | 1966 |
| Arizona | 1960 | Wyoming | 1966 |
| Colorado | 1962 | Oklahoma | 1967 |
| Michigan | 1962 | Pennsylvania | 1968 |
| New York | 1962 | Rhode Island | 1969 |
| New Hampshire | 1963 | Maryland | 1970 |
| Connecticut | 1965 | | |

## UNIFICATION OF THE LOWER COURTS IN THE STATES: ONE TIER ESTABLISHED

The following three states have attained lower-court unification by creating a single level of such positions. This pattern accords with Pound's revised model. (See Fig. 1-4.)

**Figure 1-4: The Extent of Pattern Three Adoptions**

| State | Year |
|---|---|
| Hawaii | 1959 |
| Maine | 1961 |
| North Carolina | 1962 |

## UNIFICATION BY THE ABOLITION OF ALL LOWER COURTS

Only Illinois has abolished its lower courts. In its new constitution of 1970, it retained this form of consolidation.

## CONSIDERATION OF STUDIES OF LOWER-COURT UNIFICATION

Several studies were conducted in the states to assess the possibility of lower-court unification in some form. The most publicized ones were undertaken in Rhode Island (1967),[24] Maryland (1967),[25] South Carolina (1971),[26] and Tennessee (1971).[27] All of these investigations led to the recommendation that the third pattern of unification (one tier) be followed. Such reorganizations have followed in Maryland and South Carolina.

## PATTERNS OF UNIFICATION PROGRESS AFTER 1971

The same five-part typology is applicable to the latest efforts at lower-court unification in the states. The volume of available data entails a separation of the 1971–73 patterns from the earlier ones.

## LOWER-COURT CHANGES SHORT OF UNIFICATION

So far at least four states have undertaken alterations of their lower courts without unifying them statewide.

*Wyoming (1971):* In 1971, the legislature in this state authorized the supreme court to exercise supervisory powers over justices of the peace by 1975.[28]

*Indiana (1973):* Two proposed changes are noteworthy. One was that a bill to abolish the justice-of-the-peace offices cleared the state senate but not the house of representatives. The other was that the power of the state court administrator to assign judicial personnel was increased.[29]

*Rhode Island (1973):* A judicial council with broad assignment power was created. Earlier state trial-court unification with a single level of minor courts was proposed. In addition, legislation was introduced to shift most court-related positions from a patronage basis to the state civil service system.[30]

*New York (1973):* The Temporary Commission on the New York State Court System urged a partial unification of the ten lower courts (the county courts, court of claims, family court, surrogate's court, district courts, town courts, city courts, village courts, and New York City criminal and civil courts). The commission recommended that "there should be a statewide court of general original jurisdiction called the superior court. . . . The present supreme court [the general trial court in this state], court of claims, county court, surrogate's court, and family court should be merged into the superior court."[31] The district, town, city, and New York City courts would remain as tribunals of limited jurisdiction. Moreover, this study group urged the creation of a chief administrative judge appointed by the chief judge of the Court of Appeals (the tribunal of last resort) and charged with managerial responsibility for the entire state court system. This administrator would be empowered to appoint four deputies: one for administrative services, one for inter-mediate appellate court services, one for the trial courts outside New York City, and one for the trial courts within this metropolis. Legislation incorporating these ideas was proposed. Finally, in November, 1973, a minor unification measure (a merger of the Nassau County Court into the state supreme court) failed to achieve ratification by the voters.[32]

## PARTIAL UNIFICATION OF THE LOWER COURTS IN THE STATES: TWO OR MORE TIERS PRESERVED

Four states have made reductions in the number of lower courts within their existing framework of two or more tiers.

*Minnesota (1972):* In November, 1972, a constitutional amendment consolidating the county and probate courts throughout the state (except for the three largest counties) was ratified.[33]

*Idaho (1972):* The magistrate divisions of the district courts were authorized to assume the jurisdiction of three abolished lower courts: probate, justice, and municipal tribunals.

*Ohio (1973):* A constitutional amendment was approved by the voters at the November election to permit the municipal courts to become a division of the county courts of common pleas and to allow multicounty court districts.

*Alabama (1973):* On December 18, 1973, the voters of this state overwhelmingly approved a new judicial article which reduced the number of lower courts from nineteen to three: district, probate, and municipal. In addition, the state supreme court was accorded rule-making power over such courts as well as the right to transfer their judges temporarily to other courts. The chief justice of the Alabama Supreme Court, Howell T. Heflin, was a primary advocate of this change and expects to appoint advisory committees to help effect the new article. This ratification culminates several years of judicial ferment in Alabama. For instance, in 1971, the legislature granted civil rule-making authority to the supreme court, established a state court administrator's office, and permitted the short-term assignment of judges. The new article incorporates these changes and gives them constitutional (rather than merely legislative) protection. In 1972, the voters consented to the abolition of the justice-of-the peace office and approved the creation of a judicial commission to discipline and remove judges.[34]

## UNIFICATION OF THE LOWER COURTS IN THE STATES: ONE TIER ESTABLISHED

Two states have moved toward the creation of a single tier of lower courts.

*Florida (1972–73):* On March 14, 1972, the voters in this state ratified a new judicial article, which became effective on January 2, 1973, and consolidated all limited jurisdictional courts into circuit courts (general trial courts) and county courts, the new statewide lower-court system. Twenty circuit courts abolished the functions of 120 justices of the peace, 67 county judge's courts, 46 small claims courts, 21 county courts, 12 juvenile courts, 6 types of courts of record in 21 counties, 4 magistrate's courts, and the metropolitan courts of Dade and Duvan counties. The lone exception to this absorption was the municipal courts, to be eliminated gradually before January 3, 1977. So far nine cities (Bradenton, Fort Myers, Fort Walton Beach, Miami, New Port Richey, Pensacola, St. Petersburg, Sanford, and Tampa) have abolished municipal courts. An acceleration of this process was proposed before the legislature and is still pending.[35]

*Nebraska (1972):* On March 30, 1972, the legislature in this state established a uniform system of county courts that absorbed the jurisdiction of three lower tribunals: justice-of-the-peace, police magistrate's, and old county tribunals. The new law allowed only one such court per county. The district court still remained the trial court of general original jurisdiction.[36]

## UNIFICATION BY THE ABOLITION OF ALL LOWER COURTS

Four states have abolished at least temporarily all their lower courts. The state legislatures may still create a uniform system of such tribunals to replace them but have not yet taken this step. These states are: Kansas (1972); South Dakota (1972); South Carolina (1972); and Iowa (1973).[37]

## CONSIDERATION AND STUDIES OF LOWER-COURT UNIFICATION

Numerous court studies in the various states have either been completed recently or are still in progress. The finished reports generally advocate a form of court unification with a single level of lower courts (pattern 3). These reports center on twenty-five states.

*California (1971):* That year, the consulting firm of Booz, Allen, and Hamilton, Inc.[38] and the Select Committee on Trial-Court Delay[39] published comprehensive reports endorsing judicial unification in either of two forms: the merger of the municipal and justice courts into a single tribunal, or the absorption of their functions by the superior courts (the general trial courts) whose original jurisdiction would be expanded from felonies and civil suits exceeding $5,000 in claims to an unlimited status in both categories. Although such consolidation was not proposed between 1950 (the year of the last overhaul of the California trial-court system) and 1969, every legislative session since 1970 has witnessed the introduction of legislation to allow the state or the county to place all trial-court jurisdiction in one organization. None of these proposals has come close to passage by the legislature.

*Tennessee (1971-72):* In this state two studies have recommended the establishment of a uniform system of lower courts. To date no legislative action has been taken on such a proposal.[40]

*Texas (1971-75):* During the last few years the ferment for court unification in this state has been widespread. Although numerous studies differ greatly in this respect, a typology of the recommendations toward this subject is possible. One class of studies advocates the creation of a single lower-court tier (county or justice-of-the-peace courts) to replace the seven kinds of limited jurisdictional tribunals now in existence: the juvenile courts, courts of domestic relations, county courts, probate courts, county courts of law, justice-of-the-peace, and municipal courts. The leading advocates of this change are the Chief Justice's Task Force for Court Improvement and state representative L. Dewitt Hale, the chairman of the house judiciary committee which has been examining the Texas court system since 1970. In 1973, a judicial article containing this proposal was introduced in the state legislature. The second category embraces the advocacy of unification with two lower-court levels: county and justice courts. The foremost proponent of this idea is the Texas Constitutional Revision Commission. Both kinds of proposals were considered by the state legislature which, in early 1974, sat as a constitutional convention and nearly adopted the second unification approach.[41]

*Louisiana (1972-74):* During these years the judiciary of this state was examined by the Institute of Judicial Administration and the American Judicature Society, both of which urged the creation of a single level of limited jurisdictional tribunals. However, in 1973, the state constitutional convention refused to accept this recommendation. Instead, the new judicial article written by this convention removes the constitutional status from six kinds of lower courts (justices-of-the-peace, constables, city courts, juvenile tribunals, municipal courts, and the specialized courts—municipal and traffic—in New Orleans) and permits the state legislature to abolish or combine them. The proposed article created a framework for such unification and won popular ratification (by 57.8% of the vote) on April 20, 1974. This proposal also empowers the state supreme court to make rules for the entire judiciary, to exercise general supervisory powers, and to permit the chief justice to shift judicial personnel from one tribunal to another.[42]

*Rhode Island (1972):* This state features a general trial court (the superior court) and two lower tribunals (the district and family courts). Although judicial reorganization reduced the number of district organizations from twelve to seven, the committee on court structure in this state has advocated a unification of all three courts on a county-by-county basis, beginning with Kent, Newport, and Washington counties. So far this recommendation has not been carried out.[43]

*Arizona (1973):* The feasibility of lower-court unification (along with statewide court financing and a state judicial civil service) is being investigated by the Administrative Office of the Courts and the State Legislative Council and is expected to be finished by early 1974.[44]

*Kansas (1973):* At the behest of the Chief Justice of the Kansas Supreme Court, Harold R. Fatzer, the Institute of Judicial Administration conducted an examination of the state court system, including the matter of judicial unification. The study was finished in the spring of 1974. Although the voters in 1972 ratified a constitutional amendment eliminating all constitutional references to lower courts, a proposed new judicial article would provide solely for district courts as the general trial courts and let the legislature decide whether to provide for branches of the district courts or set up a uniform system of lower courts.[45]

*Kentucky (1973):* The Kentucky Citizens for Judicial Improvement, Inc. has advocated the abolition of the lower courts in this state (county, quarterly, justice's, police, fiscal, and classes one through six of the city tribunals) and their replacement by a single level of district courts. This provision is contained in a judicial article that was introduced in the 1974 legislative session and ratified by the electorate in 1975. It resulted from a study of the state court system by the Court Studies Division of the National College of the State Judiciary in Reno, Nevada.[46]

*Michigan (1973):* This state contains at least five kinds of lower courts: district courts, the Court of Common Pleas in Detroit, the Superior Court of Grand Rapids, municipal courts, and probate tribunals. Two pieces of relevant legislation have been introduced and are still pending. One would create a uniform statewide set of limited courts by requiring the district courts to absorb the functions of the other specialized tribunals. The other bill is far more modest since it would merely phase out the remaining twenty-eight municipal courts by 1977 and transfer their jurisdiction to the district courts. Moreover, in 1972, the Special Commission to Review Article VI recommended the absorption of probate jurisdiction by the general trial courts (the circuit courts), which would also assume the tasks of the recorder's court in Detroit. In December, 1973, the nationally respected consulting firm of Ernst and Ernst finished its studies of the Michigan judiciary, examining the best ways of implementing such proposed legislation if passed.[47]

*New Hampshire (1973):* A study by the Institute of Judicial Administration urged that this state combine all of its lower courts into a single set of district courts. So far this recommendation has not resulted in legislative action.[48]

*Oregon (1973):* The Governor's Commission on Judicial Reform has endorsed the concept of lower-court unification by urging that the state legislature should be empowered to create, modify, or eradicate all tribunals below the supreme court level. However, the only resulting legislative action has been the passage of a bill enlarging the chief justice's administrative powers over the limited jurisdictional courts (county, municipal, and justice-of-the-peace).[49]

*Utah (1973):* Although a lower-court unification bill was introduced in the 1972 session of the Utah legislature, it remained in the judiciary committee of both houses. The only portion of the proposed measure that was passed was a provision creating an Administrative Office of the Courts.[50]

*Washington (1973):* During the last few years, the Citizens Conference on Washington Courts has been the most active group urging minor-court unification in this state. In 1973, its suggestions became part of a proposed constitutional amendment to eliminate all lower courts and permit the state legislature to create a set of district courts or to let the superior court, as a general trial court, handle the cases formerly adjudicated in the minor courts. This suggested judicial article is undergoing revisions by the state senate judiciary committee.[51]

*West Virginia (1973–74):* In 1973 and 1974, constitutional amendments were introduced to permit the legislature to establish a single layer of tribunals to replace its lower courts—justice-of-the-peace and county courts. Under both proposals the supreme court would exercise supervisory, rule-making, personnel-assignment, and budgetary powers over all judicial levels. A legislative attempt was then made to reduce the number of the justice-of-the-peace offices. In 1974, the people of the state voted to abolish them.[52]

*Wisconsin (1973):* The Citizens Study Committee on Judicial Organization has called for the elimination of all lower courts (county and municipal tribunals) in Wisconsin and the absorption of their duties by a single kind of trial court with general original jurisdiction. However, a proposal before the state legislature in 1973 sought to permit this branch to create a single layer of minor courts (municipal courts) if it wanted. This measure also would empower the chief justice of the supreme court to appoint the chief judges of each general trial court (the circuit courts) and to exercise extensive control over trial-court operations.[53]

*Vermont (1974):* In March, 1974, the voters in this state decided the fate of several proposed judicial amendments that would create a unified court system with a general trial court, the superior court, and with whatever lower courts, if any, the legislature establishes. Moreover, this series of proposals furnishes constitutional protection for the rule-making power of the state supreme court.[54]

*Other States:* In addition, nine other states have devoted much attention to lower-court unification. Studies centering on this topic are still in progress in Georgia and Virginia. Arkansas (1965), Indiana (1967), and Mississippi (1970) have finished studies recommending such change. It might be added that in the Hoosier state, the justice-of-the-peace tribunals are expected to be phased out of existence by 1976 and that in January, 1974, legislation was proposed to establish a single set of lower tribunals for almost every county. Recent attempts at minor-court unification have failed in four states: North Dakota (1972), Nevada (1972), and Montana (1972), by the voters' rejections of constitutional amendments, and in New York (1972) by legislative inaction on Governor Nelson Rockefeller's proposal.

But all told, thirty-one states—twenty-one during the 1946-70 period and ten during the 1971-73 span—have achieved a form of lower-court unification in accordance with the second, third, or fourth patterns. In most states, the implementation of such change has taken from one to three years.

## A FORECAST AND POSTSCRIPT

A prognosis of lower-court unification in the states centers on at least three issues: an attempt to predict the year when every state will have achieved one form of such consolidation, a consideration of forces that might accelerate this development, and some limitations on the unification trend.

First, the only public forecast on this subject belongs to R. Stanley Lowe, Associate Director of the American Judicature Society, who recently commented:

At the beginning of this century, every state in the union had a proliferated, overlapping court system, instituted after the Revolution and patterned after the 500-year-old English pattern [*sic*]. At this writing [early 1973], [numerous] states have implemented Roscoe Pound's ideal of a single, structured court divided into two or three levels, one to handle the appellate business and one or two for trial work. Many more states have taken significant steps in this direction. It is not unreasonable to project that before the end of this decade [1979], unified systems will have been instituted in all 50 states.[55]

If one assumes that all the states will install the second, third, or fourth patterns of lower-court unification, that is, one of these three forms, Lowe's impressionistic forecast is probably too optimistic. A quantitative analysis disputes his contention.

Figure 1-5 presents a summation of the progress toward lower-court unification. If all of the states were to follow only the second pattern

Figure 1-5: Progress in Lower-Court Unification

|  | Year Span | Unification Pattern | | | |
|---|---|---|---|---|---|
|  |  | Pattern 2 | Pattern 3 | Pattern 4 | Total |
|  | 1947–60 | 4 ( 80%) | 1 (20%) | 0 ( 0%) | 5 (100%) |
|  | 1961–65 | 7 ( 70%) | 2 (20%) | 1 (10%) | 10 (100%) |
|  | 1966–70 | 6 (100%) | 0 ( 0%) | 0 ( 0%) | 6 (100%) |
|  | 1971–73 | 4 ( 40%) | 2 (20%) | 4 (40%) | 10 (100%) |
| Total: | 1947–73 | 21 ( 68%) | 5 (16%) | 5 (16%) | 31 (100%) |

(the modal preference), they would probably achieve this form of unification between 1993 and 1995, depending on the base year chosen for calculations on an assumption of constancy in the rate of change. If the states were to adopt the third model (directly or in evolution from Pattern 2), this prospect is likely to take place by 2041. If the states were to follow the fourth pattern, they would probably accomplish it by 2007. These projections are estimates, mainly because they posit that specified rates of development will persist indefinitely.

However, these calculations suggest that all the states will eventually adopt one of these models. If one views these patterns as evolutionary developments rather than as mutually exclusive alternatives, it is reasonable to project that every state is likely to have adopted lower-court unification in one form or another between 1979 and 1989. This estimate again depends on the arithmetical premises that one accepts.

Second, this goal may be achieved by the 1980s only because of recent progress and the scope of current efforts but also because of indirect pressure from the United States Supreme Court, which overturned a conviction in an Ohio mayor's court (a fee office) on the ground that the defendant was denied a trial before an impartial judge as guaranteed by the due process clause of the Fourteenth Amendment.[56] Since court unification *ipso facto* necessitates the elimination of fee offices, this ruling may supply impetus toward unification in some states.

Some legal scholars have recently suggested that, even if the states do achieve a form of lower-court unification, the judicial system, although much improved, will still be defective mechanisms for the peaceful resolution of social conflicts. One widely respected analyst, Francis C. Cady, recently commented:

A conclusion of discussion relative to proposals for modernization of the [state] judicial system, [*sic*] emphasizes that even the ideal judicial system cannot cope with all the societal problems that are being heaped upon the shoulders of our judges today.[57]

In short, an improvement in the structure and administration of the state courts, particularly at the trial level, may only postpone the day when judges, legislators, and other members of the legal profession will have to consider seriously a substantial reduction in the scope of judicial functions.

Nonetheless, a unification of the lower courts in all of the states is probably imminent. The capture of this judicial Holy Grail that Pound first pursued may soon be at hand. It will be a significant step toward achieving a justice system that is skillful, efficient, evenhanded, and fair. But such reorganization is not the whole answer. Even Pound cautioned:

Unification of the [state] courts will not do everything. There must be judges equal to their tasks and unafraid to do them. The mode of selection and tenure must be such as to insure such judges as far as may be. But no judges can achieve results such as are demanded today if they are held to the machinery of the last century. Things are done by the combined working of men and machinery. In that combination machinery is given them to work with. But our ideal must be the right men with the right machinery.[58]

Finally, as a postscript, recent, salient court developments in Kentucky and Texas deserve mention. Both states have made serious moves toward revamping the structural and operational aspects of their judicial systems.

On November 4, 1975, Kentucky became the thirty-second state to unify its courts (and, concomitantly, to abolish its justices of the peace) when voters ratified a new judicial amendment to the state constitution. The final margin of adoption, according to James G. Amato (Executive Director of the Kentucky Citizens for Judicial Improvement, Inc., a strong proponent of the measure) was 212,631 in favor and 178,987 opposed. Although this 54.2% edge represented a narrow victory, even some supporters were reportedly surprised. Voter approval was significant, particularly in view of the overhauling that the new article required over several years, beginning on January 1, 1976. From the standpoint of unification, this amendment essentially eliminated a spate of lower courts, including quarterly, county, justice's, police, and fiscal tribunals and encompassing at least twelve hundred judges. Replacing them in January, 1978, will be a statewide network of district courts with the circuit courts remaining as general trial courts. Such tribunals will become part of "one [statewide] Court of Justice" managed by a new court of last resort.

However, the reduction of lower courts to a single tier is merely one long-advocated standard for measuring the extent of unification. Such criteria date from the time of legal scholar Roscoe Pound in the early 1900s. Among such desiderata are the following: the role of the chief justice of the new state supreme court (replacing the old court of appeals, which becomes an intermediate appellate body) as the executive head of the entire state judicial system; his constitutional authority to "appoint such administrative assistants as he deems necessary . . . [and] perform all other necessary administrative functions relating to the court"; the right to submit to the legislature a single proposed budget for the whole state court system; and broad powers to make temporary assignments of judicial personnel from one court to another in order to expedite the flow of cases. It is not clear whether this last form of authority extends to court-support personnel. Finally, the new court of last resort is accorded much latitude in making administrative and other rules for the state judiciary *in toto.*[59]

By contrast, on the same November day, the people of Texas overwhelmingly defeated a proposed judicial article, although, according to Jim Hutcheson (Chief Counsel of the Texas Judicial Council), the "Judiciary proposition . . . polled the best of the eight propositions on the ballot." The final margin of loss was reported as 830,342 against (71.7%) and 327,713 in favor (28.3%). What makes a comparison of results in both states singularly appropriate is that the proposed judicial amendments were almost identical with respect to the unification features, except that the Texas measure did not provide for state court budgeting. The conflicting results probably stemmed not from ideological differences in the two state electorates but from the degree of political support for the respective articles. Unlike Kentucky, Texas was sharply divided over this and other constitutional proposals. In fact, some legislators, along with Governor Dolph Briscoe and Criminal Appeals Court Presiding Judge John Onion, publicly opposed all eight measures. This setback negated a three-year effort to restructure the state court system. The huge margin of defeat and the uncertain reelection prospects of some legislators who campaigned for the propositions make the future of judicial reform in this state problematical.[60]

# 2

# DEVELOPMENTS IN
# STATE COURT FINANCING

> *. . . the [Supreme] Court once again earnestly urges imme-
> diate action by the legislature to finance the court system
> [of Michigan] on the only practical, sensible basis—state-
> wide, to do away once and for all with the fragmented, un-
> fair system which has made a mockery of Michigan's "one
> court of justice," as intended in the Constitution [and]
> to provide [the] means for management reorganization of
> the entire system. . . .*[1]

Thomas M. Kavanagh, Chief Justice of the Michigan Supreme Court,
made this comment in delivering a state-of-the-judiciary speech to a joint
session of the Michigan legislature. His statement exemplifies growing
sentiment among judicial administrators and scholars for the state assumption of all costs, regardless of court level or type of expense. It represents
an attempt by state supreme courts to improve their supervision of the
entire judicial system through budgetary control and to join their legislative and executive counterparts as a genuine department of state government. Furthermore, this trend is a segment of a far larger movement—
the unification of the numerous trial courts in the states under the direction of their highest tribunal, its chief justice, or a judicial council. Such
consolidation embraces at least four areas: the right of the state supreme
court to make rules for the entire judicial system; the authority of this
body or its head to assign judges and court-related employees temporarily
from one tribunal to another; its right to establish a classification system
for judicial personnel at all levels; and its power to formulate a single
budget for the entire judiciary.

030738

This section centers upon the fourth area, analyzing salient aspects of state court financing. More specifically, the topic of state court finance consists of four aspects: (1) preliminary matters, including definition of state court financing, the significance of this widely proposed change, and the methods of centralized financing available to state courts; (2) the progress toward such a cost takeover; (3) the main provisions for judicial expenses; and (4) a prognosis.

## PRELIMINARIES

### A DEFINITION OF STATE COURT FINANCING

*State court financing* denotes the right of the state judicial department to pay for its operating and capital costs at all levels (trial and appellate) through a single annual budget prepared by the supreme court (or one of its agents, such as the chief justice or the state court administrator and the latter's aides), submitted directly to the legislature for its consideration (without review by the executive branch), passed with or without alterations, and enacted by gubernatorial signature or a legislative override. All money raised by the courts of the state would be deposited in the state treasury (or general fund). Three notable limitations on this broad definition have evolved. First, state court financing is considered to prevail when 90 percent or more of the yearly judicial costs are paid by the state. Second, revenues derived from traffic fines and local ordinance violations may be kept by the municipalities in which the offenses have taken place. Third, sometimes the state will initially pay for the costs of judicial facilities but later charge the local governmental units (usually cities or counties) for such expenditures.

### THE SIGNIFICANCE OF STATE COURT FINANCING

Proposals for state court financing are significant because they are a feature of the court-unification movement. The annual (or biennial) preparation of a budget for the entire state judiciary is a central task facing the chief justice of the state supreme court, along with his other principal managerial responsibilities: the formation and promulgation of rules for uniform practices and procedures, the assignment of judges and other employees from one court to another, and the establishment and maintenance of a personnel-classification system. The chief justice oversees the performance of these duties in regular consultation with his colleagues on the supreme court and with the advice of the judicial council, which is made up of trial- and intermediate-appellate judges, lawyers, and laymen. He delegates the execution of these responsibilities to the state judicial administrator and his staff, who would be expected to work closely with trial-court executives. The duties of trial-court executives encompass calendar management, office and housekeeping operations, the supervision of auxiliary personnel (bailiffs, clerks, reporters, probation officers, and secretaries), as well as the initiation of the judicial budgetary process. Recently the Institute of Judicial Administration summarized the court finance procedure as follows:

> The process of developing an overall, comprehensive budget for the courts should begin with the most basic operating unit and proceed upward. Each unit, then each court, should project its resource needs. Each forecast should be reviewed by the [state] Judicial Administrator working under the Chief Justice's auspices and a coordinated plan achieved that can be expressed in program terms. After the total judicial program has been developed in this manner, an integrated judicial budget should be presented directly to the legislature for review and funding.[2]

## METHODS OF CENTRALIZED FUND-RAISING

Three methods of state court financing merit at least brief attention because of their widespread use: a single annual (or biennial) judicial-department budget; the resort to writ of mandamus on the state treasury by the supreme court and other tribunals as an exercise of their claims to inherent powers; and a constitutionally dedicated fund. The first method is gaining currency and probably will become dominant in the states. The second means has been occasionally employed, as state courts at all levels have claimed an inherent right to obtain the funds reasonable and necessary for them to perform the functions required by the state constitution or by legislation. This contention, a variation of the separation-of-powers doctrine, has been couched in the rhetoric of judicial independence from the other branches of state government (the executive and the legislature), although the enduring reality has been their interdependence in practice. When the contention of judicial independence has been raised, it has usually centered on monetary disputes between parts of the state judicial system and local governmental units. In the few court cases between the state courts and the other two segments of state government, the issues according to legal scholar Geoffrey Hazard and his colleagues, have "always been specific, narrow, and relatively minor."[3] This method has been employed in downward vertical disputes rather than in horizontal disagreements among the three constitutionally equal sectors of government. This contention has persisted mainly because the other branches do not deem worthwhile a protracted struggle with the state judiciary over small amounts of money, not because these counterparts cannot do so. Most judicial attempts to secure funds for operations are pursued by negotiation and compromise rather than by trying to assert the judiciary's inherent powers through writs of mandamus. A third method of centralized judicial funding is a constitutionally dedicated fund whereby a specified portion (perhaps three or four percent) of the state budget would be earmarked for judicial use. Presumably the state judicial system would receive additional funds, if any, only as a result of bargaining with the governor and the legislature. So far this idea has been proposed only in Michigan. If enacted, this proposal would greatly improve the availability of judicial funds in most states, where the typical judicial portion of the state budget amounts to less than one percent and in no event to more than two percent.[4]

In addition, at least eight other judicial devices exist for obtaining funds: declaratory judgments, which often accompany writs of mandamus; contempt proceedings against state budgetary officials who fail to comply with court financial orders; debt actions by unpaid judicial employees against the state or counties; debt actions by court suppliers; suits by sheriffs' offices for reimbursement of funds spent under court order for judicial purposes; taxpayer suits to forbid or require public expenditures for specific court purposes; direct *ex parte* orders to proscribe any interference with court operations; *quo warranto* to bar changes in judicial-budget estimates; and eviction orders for needed court facilities. However, these methods have rarely been used, first, because judicial financial requests are regularly fulfilled and ultimately, because courts, as agencies virtually devoid of coercive powers, fear the issuance of orders that may be defied by the executive or legislative branches.[5]

## THE MOMENTUM OF FISCAL CHANGE

A consideration of state court financing from the perspectives of definition, significance, and alternatives is a prelude to an examination of its momentum, which has been fueled by numerous sources. The National

Municipal League (1963), the President's Commission on Law Enforcement and the Administration of Justice (1967), the National Conference on the Judiciary (1971), the Advisory Commission on Intergovernmental Relations (1971), the Institute for Court Management in Denver (1971), the Committee on Economic Development (1972), the National Commission on Criminal Justice Standards and Goals (1973), the American Judicature Society, and the Institute for Judicial Administration have been among the long-standing proponents of such financing. The ultimate rationale for this change is that it contributes to the attainment of a state judicial system that is competent, fair, consistent, and effective in its disposition of civil and criminal cases.[6]

From this ultimate justification stem numerous reasons which may be classified into four groups: general purpose, institutional, administrative, and fiscal. Among the general reasons are the responsibility of the state to attempt to upgrade the judicial system; the discharge of constitutionally mandated and statutory obligations; and the view of judicial services as state responsibilities (although locally administered). Foremost among the institutional considerations is a desire for judicial independence from the other sectors of state government. The main administrative contentions include the attainment of a desired overview of the total cost for dispensing justice, the fear of hampering progress toward judicial unification because of state dependence on local governments to pay for trial-court operations, the need for a unitary budget as an instrument of planning, policy-making control, and coordination, and the availability of cost data for such objectives; the attainment of visibility in the flow of money through the judicial establishment; and the fear of obstruction of the chief justice's assignment power because of variations in local financing patterns for the same kind of work. Among the leading fiscal considerations are the desire to afford property-tax relief; the opportunity to use the state's broader revenue base; a tendency to relieve local governmental units of a burden that many of them cannot sustain; the desire to end the use of courts as revenue-raising devices; the effort to end the practice in some communities of reducing charges against defendants to avoid prospective costly trials; and the attitude that the disposition of cases should not rest upon the ability of a city or county to afford a trial.

One nationally respected state court administrator, Ralph N. Kleps of California, expressed the case for state court financing by pleading:

So far as our state judicial systems are concerned, all we are suggesting is the creation of a beacon light of central responsibility in a sea of localism, and we are light years away from any operating centralized judicial administration. As a matter of fact, I believe that the length to which a centralized judicial authority will be permitted to go in any state depends on two related factors. One is the degree of necessity imposed by the societal pressures of continuing system overloads and the other is the degree of competency with which a central authority actually performs its function. . . .

Throughout the United States the judicial branch of government is the least well-supported and has the most fragmented sources of financial support. In my opinion, no program for the improved operation of state judicial systems can be made upon the premise that money can be saved. You can no more save money in the design and operation of an effective, modern judicial system than you can save money in the construction of a modern highway system.[7]

The opposition to state court financing consists of total and partial components, all of which are fiscal. Total opposition rests on four ideas: that the state should not decree expenditures by local governments unless it is willing to pay for a substantial part of them; the reduced tendency of trial courts to bend toward local needs; the lost pecuniary advantages from fines and fees (principally for traffic violations); and the alleged undesirability for the state to take on an additional fiscal burden. Partial opposition centers around having the local government units continue to pay for capital costs (especially court facilities) because such buildings are typically multipurpose. They house most local operations, such as the sheriff's office, the district attorney's office, the probation department, and the public defender's office. However, the Advisory Commission on Intergovernmental Relations has countered both forms of resistance by remarking: "We are not prepared to accept a high degree of responsiveness to local needs, if it means uneven and inequitable application of the law between jurisdictions."[8]

Finally, the arguments over the desirability of state court financing have gradually lost their salience as some states have moved in this direction. The most powerful impetus for this change may come from an inclination to emulate the successful experiences of other states. So far twelve states have adopted this kind of financing: Alaska (1959), Maine (1961), Vermont (1961), North Carolina (1962), Connecticut (1965), Hawaii (1965), Rhode Island (1965), Oklahoma (1967), New Mexico (1968), Colorado (1970), Maryland (1970), and South Dakota (1972).

At least nineteen states have recently considered paying for the expenses of all courts. In six of these states, Arizona, Mississippi, New Hampshire, Oregon, South Carolina, and Tennessee, this matter has been under study recently or currently. In one state (North Dakota) this financing method was permitted by a proposed constitution, which the voters rejected in November, 1972. In the remaining twelve states, this change is being sought by legislation or by a new judicial article.

## STATES WHERE CHANGES ARE BEING SOUGHT BY LEGISLATION

*California:* During the last few years, three prominent organizations—the nationally prominent consulting firm of Booz, Allen, and Hamilton; the Select Committee on Trial Court Delay; and the Institute for Court Management—conducted studies that advocated total state court financing, except for parking fines and forfeitures which would be retained by localities. In 1972 and 1973, bills featuring this change were introduced by Assemblyman James A. Hayes (now a member of the Los Angeles County Board of Supervisors) and state senator Jack Fenton. But no measure has cleared either house of the legislature.[9]

*Florida:* A new state constitution was approved by the voters on March 14, 1972, and took effect on January 2, 1973. Although it provided for virtual state court financing, legislation has been proposed to require the state to pay the salaries of all trial court-related personnel: 3,324 employees. The foremost advocate of this additional change has been the Chief Justice of the Florida Supreme Court, Vassar B. Carlton.[10]

*Kansas:* A new judicial article permitting full state court financing was ratified by the voters of this state in November, 1972. During 1973, the legislature authorized the state supreme court to create a Judicial Advisory Study Committee to recommend laws implementing this article. This committee hired the Institute of Judicial Administration to study the feasibility of total state court financing, among other topics. The study was due for completion in 1975.[11]

*Kentucky:* In late 1973, a proposed constitutional amendment that included a state assumption of all judicial costs was submitted to the Joint Legislative Interim Committee on Elections and Constitutional Amendments. It was prepared by representatives from the Court of Appeals (the highest tribunal in this state), the Kentucky Bar Association, the Governor's Judicial Council, and the Kentucky Crime Commission. Another influential group, Kentucky Citizens for Judicial Improvement, Inc., proposed a new judicial article with the same feature. The amendments were submitted to the legislature in 1974 and ratified by the voters in 1975.[12] Because of legislative actions taken in December, 1976, the new system is expected to become fully operational in January, 1978, as originally scheduled.

*Louisiana:* Recently the court system of this jurisdiction was examined by the Institute of Judicial Administration and the American Judicature Society, both of which urged the state takeover of all judicial expenses.[13] In 1973, the state constitutional convention approved a new judicial article which permits the legislature to make this change if it desires. This proposal was ratified by the voters of the state in April, 1974.

*Massachusetts:* In the last few years bills for the partial and full state assumption of judicial costs have been introduced in the legislature. One proposal encompassed the operating and personnel expenses of the general trial courts (the superior courts) in fourteen counties of this state. The other measure was a five-year plan for a gradual state takeover of financial responsibility for all tribunals. Both proposals were sponsored by state representatives Charles P. Flaherty of Cambridge, the House Chairman of the Joint State Legislative Committee on Counties. His latter bill was developed from a recent study of the funding and budgeting practices of the Massachusetts court system by the American Judicature Society.[14]

*Michigan:* During the last several years William R. Hart (former state court administrator), a Special Commission to Review Article VI (the judicial article of the state constitution), Ernst and Ernst (a nationally respected consulting firm), and Governor William Milliken have advocated the complete state assumption of all court expenses. In 1973 and 1974, a bill was introduced to apply this change to the district courts in this state (tribunals of limited original jurisdiction) as a first step toward the goal of state court financing. This measure did not make its way through that session.[15]

*New York:* Among the strongest recent advocates of state court financing have been Nelson A. Rockefeller while governor, the New York Committee on Modern Courts, the Institute of Judicial Administration, the American Judicature Society, and the Temporary Commission on the New York State Court System. In 1973, three bills were introduced to accomplish this purpose gradually over different periods of time (five years, ten years, and one year respectively). However, as in California, the measures would reduce state aid to localities as the cost takeover proceeded. Such aid now consists of revenues from motor-vehicle registration fees and taxes as well as motor-fuel taxes. The proposed end of these subventions implies that the state favors a disguised continuation of judicial funding as local responsibility by giving municipalities and counties free judicial services with one hand while taking away their ability to defray nonjudicial expenses with the other hand. Neither bill has passed the legislature.[16]

*Pennsylvania:* In 1973, two bills were introduced in the legislature of this state to attain a higher degree of state court financing. However, both measures fell short of a full takeover. One proposal failed to encompass judicial operating and capital outlays in the trial courts. The other proposal included the first cost but not the second. Both measures died in committee.[17]

*Texas:* Several influential voices have been urging the partial or full adoption of state-court financing. L. Dewitt Hale, Chairman of the Texas House of Representatives Judiciary Committee, has urged the state payment of all judicial salaries as well as payment of all court revenues to the state treasury. However, the Chief Justice's Task Force for Court Improvement has recommended the passage of a new judicial article that would authorize full state court financing. In 1973, a proposal incorporating this concept was introduced in both houses. Such funding was also considered by the legislature as part of a proposed new constitution when its members were sitting as a constitutional convention in 1974.[18]

*Washington:* The most active group seeking a total assumption of judicial costs has been the Citizens Conference on Washington Courts. In 1973, although a bill was introduced to achieve this goal, it has never passed. The legislature may well pass it, since there is reported to be considerable interest in such a change.[19]

*Wisconsin:* Among the leading proponents of this judicial goal have been Governor Patrick J. Lucey and the Citizens Study Committee for Judicial Organization. In 1973, a bill was introduced to accomplish this objective but has not been passed. Under this legislation the state court administrator would be entrusted with devising a biennial judicial budget.[20]

## THE MAIN CATEGORIES OF JUDICIAL EXPENSE

Despite developments in the preceding nineteen states, the prevailing scheme of court financing is still a sharing of expenses between the state and local units of government. The sharing of court expenses by states and localities pervades fourteen categories. Figures 2-1 and 2-2 provide the latest available overall depiction of the state and local funding arrangements. This information was gathered by the Institute of Judicial Administration in the late 1960s, revised by the Advisory Commission on Intergovernmental Relations in 1971, and updated by the author through

1973. A detailed analysis of the sharing arrangements under each rubric reveals the following.[21]

1. Highest Court Costs: Forty-nine states pay for the cost of their highest court, except Virginia, where the state and the local government units share the financial burden.

**Figure 2-1: Categories and Sources of Judicial Funding at the State Level (1973)**

| Categories | Miscel-laneous | Local | State / Local | State | Total Local and State |
|---|---|---|---|---|---|
| 1. Highest Court Costs | 0 | 0 | 1 | 49 | 50 |
| 2. Intermediate Appellate Court Costs | 0 | 0 | 3 | 20 | 23 |
| 3. Judicial Salaries | 0 | 1 | 17 | 22 | 40 |
| 4. Nonjudicial Salaries | 0 | 5 | 14 | 22 | 41 |
| 5. Travel Expenses | 0 | 5 | 13 | 23 | 41 |
| 6. Other Expenses | 0 | 8 | 12 | 20 | 40 |
| 7. Lower-Court Expenses | 0 | 20 | 8 | 13 | 41 |
| 8. Judicial Retirement | 0 | 1 | 7 | 27 | 35 |
| 9. Judicial Council | 1 | 0 | 0 | 22 | 22 |
| 10. Judicial Conference Expenses | 1 | 0 | 0 | 26 | 27 |
| 11. State Court Administrators' Costs | 0 | 0 | 0 | 42 | 42 |
| 12. Local Trial-Court Administrators | 0 | 7 | 0 | 7 | 14 |
| 13. Construction of Court Buildings | 0 | 18 | 10 | 9 | 37 |
| 14. Maintenance of Court Buildings | 0 | 16 | 0 | 22 | 38 |

Source: Derived from the Advisory Commission on Intergovernmental Relations, *State-Local Relations in the Criminal Justice System* (Washington, D.C.: U.S. Government Printing Office, 1971), p. 110 and Appendix 1.

2. Intermediate Appellate Court Costs: Twenty states underwrite the costs of this judicial tier: Alabama, Arizona, California, Colorado, Connecticut, Florida, Georgia, Illinois, Indiana, Louisiana, Maryland, Michigan, Missouri, New Jersey, New Mexico, North Carolina, Oklahoma, Pennsylvania, Tennessee, and Texas. Only three states, Kentucky, New York, and Ohio, have state/local sharing arrangements. The remaining twenty-seven states lack an intermediate appellate court.

3. Judicial Salaries: Twenty-two states pay all judicial salaries regardless of

court level: Alabama, Alaska, Arkansas, Colorado, Connecticut, Florida, Hawaii, Idaho, Missouri, Montana, New Hampshire, North Carolina, North Dakota, Oklahoma, Oregon, Rhode Island, South Dakota, Tennessee, Utah, Vermont, Virginia, and Wyoming. However, almost as many states, seventeen, divide the costs between the state and local governments: California, Delaware, Kansas, Louisiana, Maine, Maryland, Massachusetts, Michigan, Minnesota, Mississippi, Nebraska, New Mexico, New York, Ohio, Washington, West Virginia, and Wisconsin. Only one state, Georgia, permits local governments to defray judicial salaries at all levels of the state court system. The remaining ten states did not furnish the data requested by the Institute of Judicial Administration.

**Figure 2-2: State Share of Total State/Local Judicial Expenditures (1973) in Ascending Order**

| State | Share | State | Share | State | Share |
|---|---|---|---|---|---|
| Arizona | (12%) | North Dakota | (25%) | Utah | ( 57%) |
| Ohio | (13%) | Tennessee | (26%) | Idaho | ( 57%) |
| California | (13%) | Oregon | (27%) | Delaware | ( 68%) |
| Pennsylvania | (16%) | Mississippi | (27%) | Kentucky | ( 72%) |
| Washington | (17%) | Montana | (29%) | Vermont | (100%) |
| Nevada | (17%) | Kansas | (29%) | South Dakota | (100%) |
| Michigan | (17%) | Wisconsin | (31%) | Rhode Island | (100%) |
| Georgia | (17%) | Illinois | (33%) | Oklahoma | (100%) |
| South Carolina | (18%) | New Jersey | (34%) | North Carolina | (100%) |
| Florida | (18%) | Missouri | (34%) | New Mexico | (100%) |
| Texas | (19%) | Louisiana | (35%) | Maryland | (100%) |
| Indiana | (19%) | Wyoming | (36%) | Maine | (100%) |
| New York | (20%) | Nebraska | (40%) | Hawaii | (100%) |
| Minnesota | (21%) | West Virginia | (42%) | Connecticut | (100%) |
| Massachusetts | (22%) | Virginia | (47%) | Colorado | (100%) |
| Alabama | (23%) | Arkansas | (47%) | Alaska | (100%) |
| Iowa | (24%) | New Hampshire | (51%) | | |

Source: Derived from the Advisory Commission on Intergovernmental Relations, *State-Local Relations in the Criminal Justice System* (Washington, D.C.: U.S. Government Printing Office, 1971), p. 108 and Appendix 1. Updated by the author.

4. Nonjudicial Salaries: Twenty-two states pay the nonjudicial salaries for all tiers within the state court system: Alabama, Alaska, Arkansas, Colorado, Connecticut, Florida, Hawaii, Idaho, Maryland, Missouri, Montana, New Hampshire, North Carolina, North Dakota, Oklahoma, Rhode Island, South Dakota, Tennessee, Utah, Vermont, Virginia, and Wyoming. Fourteen states divide these salary costs with local governments: Delaware, Kansas, Louisiana, Maine, Massachusetts, Michigan, Minnesota, Mississippi,

Nebraska, New Mexico, New York, Ohio, West Virginia, and Wisconsin. In five states local governments pick up the tab for such salaries: California, Georgia, Maryland, Oregon, and Washington. The remaining nine states provided no data for this item.

5. Travel Expenses: Twenty-three states pay for all judicial travel expenses: Alabama, Alaska, Arkansas, Colorado, Connecticut, Florida, Hawaii, Idaho, Kansas, Maryland, Missouri, Montana, New Hampshire, North Carolina, North Dakota, Oklahoma, Rhode Island, South Dakota, Tennessee, Utah, Vermont, Virginia, Wyoming. Thirteen states share these costs with local governmental units: Delaware, Louisiana, Maine, Massachusetts, Michigan, Minnesota, Mississippi, Nebraska, New Mexico, New York, Ohio, West Virginia, and Wisconsin. Five states allow local government to defray this expense: California, Georgia, Maryland, Oregon, and Washington. Nine states were silent on this score.

6. Other Expenses (apart from judicial salaries, nonjudicial salaries, and travel expenses): Twenty states defray miscellaneous expenses: Alabama, Alaska, Arkansas, Colorado, Connecticut, Florida, Hawaii, Missouri, Montana, New Hampshire, North Carolina, North Dakota, Oklahoma, Rhode Island, South Dakota, Tennessee, Utah, Vermont, Virginia, Wyoming. Twelve states share such costs with local government units: Delaware, Lousiana, Maine, Massachusetts, Michigan, Minnesota, Mississippi, New Mexico, New York, Ohio, West Virginia, and Wisconsin. Eight states require local governments to pay for these costs: California, Georgia, Idaho, Kansas, Maryland, Nebraska, Oregon and Washington. No completed data are available for the last ten states.

7. Lower Court Expenses: At least thirteen states defray the costs of their lower courts (tribunals of limited or special jurisdiction): Alaska, Colorado, Connecticut, Florida, Hawaii, Maine, Maryland, New Mexico, North Carolina, Oklahoma, Rhode Island, South Dakota, and Vermont. Eight states split the expenses for these courts: California, Louisiana, Mississippi, New Jersey, New Mexico, Oregon, and Virginia. Nineteen states make local governments pay these expenses: Arkansas, Georgia, Idaho, Indiana, Iowa, Kansas, Massachusetts, Minnesota, Montana, Nebraska, New Hampshire, Ohio, South Carolina, South Dakota, Tennessee, Utah, Washington, West Virginia, and Wisconsin. The remaining ten states did not supply information on this point.

8. Judicial Retirement: Twenty-seven states cover the retirement benefits paid to judges: Alaska, Arkansas, California, Colorado, Connecticut, Delaware, Florida, Georgia, Hawaii, Indiana, Kansas, Kentucky, Maryland,

Michigan, Montana, Nebraska, Nevada, New Hampshire, North Carolina, Oklahoma, Oregon, South Dakota, Tennessee, Vermont, Washington, Wisconsin, and Wyoming. Seven states divide such costs with local governments: Iowa, Louisiana, Massachusetts, New Jersey, New York, Ohio, and West Virginia. One state, North Dakota, entrusts this entire burden to local agencies. No data for the remaining fifteen states are available.

9. Judicial Council: The state defrays this expense in twenty-three states. Twenty-two states pay this cost directly: Alaska, California, Connecticut, Delaware, Florida, Georgia, Idaho, Iowa, Kansas, Kentucky, Louisiana, Maine, Massachusetts, Minnesota, Missouri, New Hampshire, North Carolina, Oregon, Rhode Island, Tennessee, Vermont, and Virginia. Only one state, Nebraska, delegates this expense to the state bar association.

10. Judicial Conference Expenses: The twenty-six states that have such an office pay for the costs of the judicial conference: Alaska, Colorado, Delaware, Idaho, Illinois, Indiana, Kansas, Kentucky, Louisiana, Maine, Maryland, Massachusetts, Michigan, Mississippi, Montana, New Jersey, New York, Oklahoma, Oregon, Rhode Island, South Dakota, Tennessee, Virginia, Washington, Wisconsin, and Wyoming. Again, Nebraska is the lone state whose bar association pays this cost.

11. State Court Administrators' Costs: The forty-one states that have set up an administrative office of the courts defray this expense. Only eight states lack this position: Georgia, Mississippi, Montana, New Hampshire, South Carolina, Texas, West Virginia, and Wyoming. Nevada established this position in 1971 but has refused to continue funding it.[22]

12. Local Trial-Court Administrators: So far seven states pay the expenses of employing such officials: Alaska, Colorado, Hawaii, Iowa, Maryland, Massachusetts, and Pennsylvania. An equal number of states entrusts this responsibility to the relevant locality: California, Delaware, Michigan, Minnesota, Ohio, Oregon, and Washington. The remaining thirty-six states do not have such offices.

13. Construction of Court Buildings: This expense rests exclusively with the state government in nine states: Alaska, Colorado, Connecticut, Florida, Hawaii, Missouri, Nevada, Rhode Island, and South Carolina. Ten states share this cost with local governments: California, Delaware, Idaho, Michigan, New Hampshire, Ohio, Oregon, Tennessee, Vermont, and Wyoming. Eighteen states force this entire expense upon the localities, regardless of court level: Arkansas, Indiana, Iowa, Kansas, Kentucky, Maine, Massachusetts, Minnesota, Nebraska, New Jersey, New York

(except for its highest tribunal, the Court of Appeals, which has its housing paid for by the state), North Carolina, North Dakota, Oklahoma, South Dakota, Virginia, Washington, and West Virginia. No data are available for the remaining thirteen states.

14. Maintenance of Court Buildings: Twenty-two states defray this expense: California, Colorado, Connecticut, Delaware, Florida, Georgia, Hawaii, Idaho, Indiana, Kentucky, Michigan, Montana, New Hampshire, New Jersey, New Mexico, Ohio, Oregon, Rhode Island, South Dakota, Tennessee, Vermont, and Wyoming. Sixteen states charge the various localities with this cost: Arkansas, Iowa, Kansas, Louisiana, Maine, Maryland, Massachusetts, Minnesota, Nebraska, New York (with the same exception as above), North Carolina, North Dakota, Oklahoma, Virginia, Washington, and West Virginia. Twelve states did not respond.

Finally, these categories of judicial expenses within the states invite two closing remarks. One is that the first dozen items enumerate judicial operating expenses whereas the last two embrace capital expenditures. A second point is that the sharing of such costs between state and local components operates so that the latter now pay an average of two-thirds of all judicial costs.

## A PROGNOSIS

This section centered so far on three salient aspects of state judicial financing: its preliminaries (definition, significance, position among fiscal alternatives), its progress, and its provisions. The one remaining facet of this growing trend in judicial administration, a prognosis of developments, deserves brief consideration.

At least three possibilities are likely. One is that a gradual state assumption of responsibility in regard to the fourteen categories of judicial expenses will continue to occur and will shorten the leap toward full state control. A second possibility is that the attainment of this goal in the states will probably occur in phases stretched over several years, although such a change could technically, if not politically, be effected within six months. In California the recommended time period is two or three years, at the end of which this mode of financing would become operational in one giant step. By contrast, in New York the generally suggested span varies from five to ten years, during which time this kind of financing would be adopted in phases. A third possibility is that the application of state judicial financing to the lower courts is the most salient part of this subject, just as the unification of the lower courts is the most critical aspect of the judicial consolidation movement. After all, such tribunals handle at least ninety percent of all civil and criminal actions and exercise a greater impact on the public than any other court does. Therefore, the significance of these courts encourages a prognosis for the assumption of state financial responsibility over them. Calculations suggest that the achievement of such funding in all of the states will probably take place between 2007 and 2027—the distant future. This prediction depends on the selection of a base year for calculation and the tendency of the change process to move at a fairly uniform rate. However, if this trend continues in the twelve states (previously examined) and if the ferment spreads to other jurisdictions, state court financing may be a reality as early as 1978.

Finally, the advocacy of this change is approaching urgency in its rhetoric. In a recent message to the Michigan legislators, Chief Justice Kavanagh told them:

We say to you that prolonging the status quo is intolerable. And, we must stress that until such time as the people of Michigan can count on essential and adequate financing of the entire state-wide court system, improvements in our courts will be limited to makeshift changes, or those generated by crisis.[23]

Although his remarks applied only to one state, they increasingly reflect the views of court executives and scholars in other jurisdictions.

# 3

# THE EMERGENCE
# OF STATE COURT
# PERSONNEL ADMINISTRATION

*Decentralization of [the] courts [in the states] was carried so far in the last century that the clerks were made independent functionaries, not merely beyond effective judicial control, but independent of any administrative supervision and guided only by legislative provisions and limitations. No one was charged with supervision of this part of the work of the courts. It was no one's business to look at it as a whole, seek to find how to make it more effective and to obviate waste and expense, and promote improvement. There is much unnecessary duplication, copying and recopying, and general prolixity of records in the great majority of our courts. In the clerical no less than on the judicial side most of our courts are like Artemus Ward's proposed military company in which every man was to be an officer and superior of every other. The judiciary is the only great agency of government which is habitaully given no control of its clerical force. Even the pettiest agency has much more control than the average state court.*[1]

This comment, made long ago by the eminent legal scholar Roscoe Pound, is significant in at least three respects. First, his statement centered on not only judicial and clerical personnel but also all court-related (or supportive) employees. Second, it described the condition of judicial personnel management in most states, a situation that did not begin to change until recently. Third, it foresaw the growing importance that such management has assumed. This area has become highly significant because it is a part of the larger movement that Pound advocated—the unification of trial courts under the direction of the highest state tribunal, its chief justice, or a judicial council. As previously mentioned, this trend consists of at least four segments: the right of the highest state court to make rules for the entire judicial system, the authority of this body to assign judges and court-related employees temporarily from one bench to another, the power to formulate a single budget for the entire judiciary, and the right to establish and maintain a court personnel system.

This section examines recent trends in the establishment and maintenance of state court personnel systems. Specifically, this topic consists of four components: (1) a review of some salient judicial personnel problems; (2) an exploration of important matters affecting court-related employees; (3) an examination of centralized court-personnel prototypes recently suggested for adoption in California and New York; and (4) some tentative conclusions on this subject.

## A REVIEW OF JUDICIAL PERSONNEL PROBLEMS

A canvass of the published research into judicial personnel administration at the state level discloses a scarcity of information, a striking situation when compared with the flood of data available on the related subjects of state court unification and financing. This information scarcity will probably end soon as numerous states undertake investigations that may result in the establishment of judicial personnel systems. Fortunately, sufficient public information does exist to undertake an analysis of this subject.

Such an examination entails a consideration of judicial and nonjudicial employees at the appellate- and trial-court levels. Experts in court administration have reached general agreement on a number of important issues: 1. Judicial employees fall under the categories of chief (or presiding) judges; judges; subordinate officials, such as commissioners, magistrates, and referees, who handle minor cases entrusted to them by chief judges. 2. Agreement extends to the functions that such personnel should perform. A chief judge should undertake adjudicative and administrative duties. Adjudicative duties embrace the disposition of cases; administrative duties include the assignment of cases to judges and monitoring of court-related personnel. In heavily populated jurisdictions, it is generally thought that a chief judge should be a full-time administrator. The foremost illustrations of this practice are the Presiding Judge of the Superior Court of Los Angeles County, who has been a full-time administrator since 1958,[2] and the Chief Judge of the Circuit Court of Cook County, who has done administrative work since 1964.[3]

3. Judges ought to decide cases on a full-time basis and make necessary preparations for this task. They should have no administrative functions.

4. Subordinate judicial personnel ought to handle only minor civil and criminal cases.

5. The mode of selecting judicial officials also reflects considerable agreement. It is generally believed that the chief justice of the state supreme court, with the approval of his colleagues, should appoint the chief judge for each trial-court district.[4] The preference for central direction is a concomitant of a unified state judicial system. However, some specialists (including some analysts for the Institute of Judicial Administration, the American Judicature Society, and the Institute for Court Management in Denver) have recently argued for the selection of this executive by his peers because more effective judicial operations at this level require considerable decentralization and because trial judges are closer to local court problems and are therefore more competent than the state supreme court to choose an effective leader.

6. For the selection of judges, almost all experts favor the application of what is generally called the "merit plan" to each tier within a state judicial system. The "merit plan" contains three features: the state bar association's compilation of a list of qualified judicial candidates; the governor's filling of court vacancies with listed personnel for one term; and the requirement that appointees may serve another term only if they are elected. In seeking continued tenure, judges may run without opposition, but they must garner a majority of the votes to retain their position.[5] The merit-plan method of selection may soon be adopted in a number of states; within the last few years, it has received legislative consideration in Florida, Illinois, Kentucky, Maryland, New York, North Dakota, Pennsylvania, and Texas. So far sixteen states have adopted this plan, while ten other jurisdictions use it on a voluntary basis. (See Figure 3-1.)

7. Subordinate judicial officials should be appointed by the chief judge, to serve at his pleasure.[6]

## COURT-RELATED EMPLOYEES

The category of court-related personnel encompasses all employees in the state judicial system other than judges. This category may be divided into two classes, supervisors and supportive employees.

## SUPERVISORY PERSONNEL

A discussion of judicial supervisory personnel begins with the office of state court administrator, almost universally considered a prerequisite for a unified state judicial system. So far at least forty-one states have established this position as a staff agency to the state supreme court.[7] This office, headed by an administrative director, is expected to perform four kinds of tasks: personnel management, financial administration, information management, and secretarial functions. The first task embraces the

**Figure 3-1: Adoption of the "Merit Plan" of Judicial Selection in the States (1973)**

| Merit Plan Adopted | Merit Plan Voluntary | Merit Plan not Adopted | |
|---|---|---|---|
| Alabama | California | Arizona | Nevada |
| Alaska | Georgia | Arkansas | North Carolina |
| Colorado | Maryland | Connecticut | North Dakota |
| Florida | Massachusetts | Delaware | Oregon |
| Idaho | New Hampshire | Hawaii | Pennsylvania |
| Indiana | New Jersey | Illinois | Rhode Island |
| Iowa | New Mexico | Kentucky | South Carolina |
| Kansas | New York | Louisiana | South Dakota |
| Missouri | Ohio | Maine | Texas |
| Nebraska | Wyoming | Michigan | Virginia |
| Oklahoma | | Minnesota | Washington |
| Tennessee | | Mississippi | West Virginia |
| Utah | | Montana | Wisconsin |
| Vermont | | | |
| **Total States:** 14 (28%) | 10 (20%) | 26 (52%) | |

Source: "State Court Progress at a Glance," *Judicature* 56 (May 1973): 427–30; Robert A. Martin, "Alabama Approves Judicial Article, Pay Raises, in Eleventh-Hour Vote," *Judicature* 56 (November 1973): 173.

establishment of position classifications, recruitment, evaluation, promotion, in-service training, and disciplinary procedures for all nonjudicial employees. The second task covers the preparation of the state judicial budget, its implementation, accounting, and auditing. The third task entails the statewide promulgation and administration of uniform requirements for record keeping, information systems, and statistical compilations. The final task is secretarial work for the state judicial council (or conferences), especially the arrangement of meetings and the dissemination of periodic reports on judicial matters. The administrative director is appointed by the chief justice of the state supreme court, to serve at his colleagues' pleasure. To assist this official is a deputy, chosen in the same manner.

The next layer of supervisory offices is the trial-court administrator and his deputy, also chosen by the chief judge to serve at his pleasure. Their duties include five kinds of work: the management of the court calendar; the administration of staff services (the clerk of the court, courtroom clerks, bailiffs, court reporters, law clerks, secretaries, probation officers, court-affiliated caseworkers, and professionals such as doctors and psychologists); personnel, financial, and records administration; secretarial tasks for trial-court judges; and liaison with the bar, the press, and local governmental agencies.[8]

Presiding judges of intermediate appellate courts may, in like manner, choose an administrator and a deputy. However, personnel at this level are of secondary importance at present because only twenty-three of the states[9] have intermediate appellate courts. If most states do eventually create such tribunals, one result will be a state judicial administrative structure modeled after what is sometimes called the "hospital plan," which has been advocated during the last few years most notably by the Chief Justice of the United States Supreme Court, Warren E. Burger. Under this plan, court administrators and their deputies at the highest, middle, and trial-court levels would provide and maintain the services and facilities essential for judges to work effectively. Like doctors, judges would be free to devote their time to the work of their profession: adjudication and preparation for adjudication. This proposal contrasts sharply with the present system of direct-line supervision of judges by a chief judge.[10]

Within the "hospital plan" itself, there is room for varying degrees of centralization, depending upon who appoints the chief judges and court-related personnel at the appellate- and trial-court levels. Although thousands of judicial structural patterns are mathematically possible based on the variety of court-related positions at different levels in the numerous localities, four models are presently discernible in the states along a centralization continuum. (See Figure. 3–2.)

*The Fragmentation Model.* The most common model, that of fragmentation, contains several notable characteristics. At the appellate level, the chief judges, the administrator, and his deputies are appointed and directed by the members of each particular court. At the trial-court level, the same pattern exists. In the courts of original jurisdiction, the dispersion is even greater because some court-related positions (such as clerks) are elective; other jobs (including bailiffs and probation officers) are filled by other local governmental units; and the remaining positions (such as law clerks, secretaries, librarians, reporters, accountants, and physicians) are chosen and regulated by the particular court as it sees fit. The selection,

## Figure 3-2: A Judicial Centralization Continuum

| Judicial Levels | Degree of Judicial Administrative Centralization | | | |
|---|---|---|---|---|
| | Fragmentation | Decentralization | Partial Decentralization | Centralization |
| 1. State Court Administrator | Yes* | Yes | Yes | Yes |
| 2. Deputy State Court Administrator | Yes | Yes | Yes | Yes |
| 3. Other State-Supreme-Court Support Personnel | Yes | Yes | Yes | Yes |
| 4. Intermediate-Appellate-Court Chief Judges | No | No, but** | No, but | Yes |
| 5. Intermediate-Appellate-Court Administrators | No | No, but | Yes | Yes |
| 6. Deputy Intermediate-Appellate-Court Administrators | No | No, but | Yes | Yes |
| 7. Other Intermediate-Appellate-Court Support Personnel | No | No, but | No, but | No; No, but; or Yes |
| 8. Chief Trial-Court Judges | No | No, but | No | Yes |
| 9. Trial-Court Administrators | No | No, but | Yes | Yes |
| 10. Deputy Trial-Court Administrators | No | No, but | Yes | Yes |
| 11. Other Trial-Court Support Personnel | No | No, but | No, but | No; No, but; or Yes |

*Yes = appointment from the highest state court.
**No, but = selection by peers subject to the rules of the highest state court.
Sources: Implicit in Fannie J. Klein and Ruth J. Witztum, *Judicial Administration— 1972-1973* (New York: The Institute of Judicial Administration, 1973), p. 726; Edward B. McConnell, "Court Administration," in *The Improvement of the Administration of Justice,* 5th ed. (Chicago: The American Bar Association, Section on Judicial Administration, 1971), pp. 13-14.

promotion, evaluation, and compensation of court personnel varies from one jurisdiction to another, many of which lack a chief (or presiding) judge. A typical illustration of a state with this dispersion is Nebraska, one of whose state court executives recently commented:

The personnel hiring in the courts of Nebraska is done entirely by the local [trial] courts. There is no state merit examination administered for the judicial branch. All benefits and salary schedules conform to the State Personnel Code, although there is no requirement to do so.[11]

Other illustrations are Indiana and Iowa.

*The Decentralization Model.* The next model is a decentralization (or collegial) pattern in which the chief judges at the appellate- and trial-court levels and their supporting personnel are chosen and governed by the other members of the particular bench in accordance with uniform, statewide rules promulgated by the highest state court, its chief justice, the state judicial administrator, or the judicial council. California, New York, and Illinois are among the foremost examples. Two other states (Kentucky and Louisiana) are considering legislation to adopt this model. Three additional states (Arizona, Kansas, and Washington) are studying this possibility.

*The Partial Centralization Model.* Another structural possiblity is a partial centralization pattern. In this model, the chief judges at every level are chosen and directed by their colleagues according to state rules, while the court administrators and supporting personnel at each level are selected and regulated by the highest state tribunal or one of its agents. This pattern is intermediate because the methods of selection and regulation are horizontal in the first instance but vertical in the second. The leading exponent of this model is Pennsylvania, which adopted it in 1968.[12]

*The Centralization Model.* The last schema is centralization in varying degrees. Under this pattern, all chief judges, court administrators, and other judicially related personnel are appointed and directed by the highest state tribunal. These employees may select their assistants from lists of candidates approved by the state judicial administrator (or cleared by him if there is no central list). Although it is theoretically possible to make all appointments and policies from the top, even the proponents of this pattern recognize that the very size of the state judicial system militates against applying this model to its limit. Furthermore, within such a model, this power may be located in a judicial council (composed of the chief justice, judges from all levels, members of the executive branch *ex officio,* legislators, lawyers selected by the state bar association governing board, and members of the public); the entire state supreme court; or the chief justice of the state supreme court as the head of the state judicial department.

The sequence of locations of the centralization model represents increasing steps in judicial administrative centralization. This pattern is probably a harbinger of future state judicial systems. It originated with

New Jersey in 1947[13] and was refined by Colorado in 1962 and 1966.[14] It rests upon the cardinal assumption that, since responsibility for the functioning of the state court system belongs to its highest tribunal, appointive and regulatory authority over the entire state judiciary should be located in this body. This model has been endorsed by the American Judicature Society in 1963, the National Conference on the Judiciary in 1971, the American Bar Association in 1973, and the National Advisory Commission on Criminal Justice Standards and Goals in 1973. (In 1972, however, the Institute for Court Management and the Institute of Judicial Administration[15] questioned whether this model might engender resistance at the lower judicial levels and consequent ineffectiveness for lack of wholehearted cooperation.) Nevertheless, at least nine states have adopted or are considering this approach. They include Florida, Maryland, Michigan, Rhode Island, South Carolina, Vermont, Wisconsin, California and New York. These last two states deserve further consideration because they rank first and second in national population.

## SUPPORTIVE PERSONNEL

No consensus exists as to what constitutes the scope of supportive judicial personnel. Although lists of such employees are common, a surprising fact is the lack of criteria underlying the inclusion of these positions, which are merely cited as if the reasons for mentioning them were self-evident. It is a matter of speculation whether the rationale for inclusion is principally functional, philosophical, political, or financial.

Supervisory employees are considered to be primary administrative personnel. The court officials in this class are responsible for the appointment of four categories of supportive personnel, including confidential employees, (such as law clerks and secretaries; professional personnel, such as accountants, appraisers, caseworkers, mental-health information officials, physicians, probation officers, and psychologists; technical employees, such as bailiffs, clerks of court and their deputies, courtroom clerks, court librarians, and court reporters; and miscellaneous personnel, such as a board of law examiners, a commission on judicial conduct, a committee on admissions, a committee on judicial character and fitness, a committee on uniform state laws, grand juries, jury commissioners, a law-reporting bureau, pretrial-services employees, and public administrators.

This list is a variation of the latest recommendations of the American

Bar Association and the Temporary Commission on the New York State Court System.[16] The justification for this method of classification probably stems from a widespread desire within the judicial branch of state government to increase its autonomy from the legislative and executive segments of state government and from units of local government by absorbing as many court-related services as possible. Illustrative of this attitude are the views of Ralph N. Kleps, the nationally respected Director of the Administrative Office of the California Courts:

. . . our history and the history of nearly every state is that supporting staff for the Superior Courts [one of three main trial courts] is derivative. It comes from the County Clerk; it comes from the sheriff; it comes from wherever, and I have never understood how you can get an organized decently administered system with such fragmented responsibility over the personnel.[17]

The only hesitation about absorbing as many support functions as possible under judicial control centers around probation services, especially the function of postsentencing oversight. However, even this area is finally resolved in favor of inclusion. For instance, the Report of the Temporary Commission on the New York State Court System commented:

Of the probation functions described . . . postsentence supervision is least related to the courts, and the suggestion to sever this function and place it alone within the executive [branch of the state government] has strong initial appeal. However, this would fragment the probation agencies, thereby weakening them, and would limit the flexibility inherent in having one staff perform both functions.[18]

## CENTRALIZED COURT-PERSONNEL PROTOTYPES: AN EXAMINATION

Recommendations for the adoption of highly centralized judicial personnel prototypes have recently been made in the two most populous states: California and New York.

### THE CALIFORNIA MODEL

In late 1971, a nationally known consulting firm (Booz, Allen, and Hamilton) published a study of the judicial system in California. Among its numerous recommendations was the adoption of a highly centralized judicial personnel pattern. Figure 3-3 shows how the proposed judicial structure would look.

**Figure 3-3: Proposed California Judicial Administration Structure**

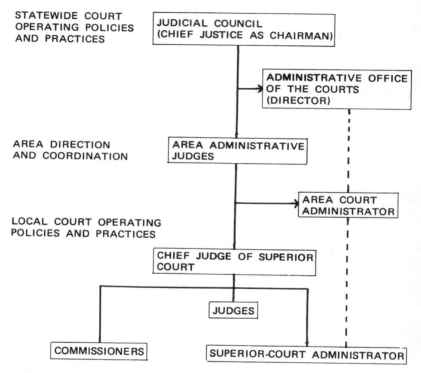

Solid lines show reporting relationships.
Dotted lines show functional relationships.

Source: Adapted from *California Unified Trial Court Feasibility Study* (San Francisco: Booz, Allen and Hamilton, Inc., 1971).

This figure contains several noteworthy aspects.

First, the Judicial Council would remain the chief policymaker for the courts of California if they were fully unified. This agency would still be composed of representatives from all judicial levels, as well as the legislature.

Second, it would continue to appoint the personnel for its staff arm, the Administrative Office of the Courts, which would conduct the research necessary for effective policy determination and implementation.

Third, the state judicial system would consist of five administrative areas (North, Central, South, Los Angeles, and the San Francisco Bay Area), each of which would contain an administrative judge and an area court administrator. These regional subdivisions were based upon geographical consideration, especially the desire to assure the reasonable proximity of courts to people and the establishment of judicial areas with approximately equal caseloads. The span of managerial control (the number of chief superior-court judges reporting directly to the area administrative judges) is probably realistic, although it varies greatly from thirty-two in the sparsely populated north region to one in the Los Angeles sector. This disparity is explained by noting that the time used in the brief conversations with all of these north-area chief judges will approximate the extensive time consumed in discussions with the chief judge of the Los Angeles County Superior Court alone. The administrative judge would be authorized by the legislature, would primarily be used to assist the chief justice of the state supreme court, would be appointed by that official for a renewable one-year term, and would receive a salary equivalent to that of an intermediate appellate-court (that is, District Court of Appeals) judge. The area court administrator would be similarly authorized, would be expected mainly to aid his area's administrative judge, and would be charged secondarily with helping the superior-court (trial-court) administrators in his area. It should be noted that the duties of the administrative judges might be entrusted to an area court administrator, but the position of administrative judge is often preferable in order to make the new system more acceptable to judges, who may fear that authority over court operations would gradually be taken out of their hands.

Fourth, the chief judge of each trial court would be appointed by the chief justice of the supreme court and would be entrusted with overseeing the performance of six tasks, including balancing caseloads among superior-court judges, associate superior-court judges (formerly municipal-court judges), and commissioners; developing local-court plans consistent with statewide policies; directing staff-support activities; identifying and correcting judicial problems; planning and controlling ongoing trial-court management; and selecting and training commissioners.

Fifth, the superior-court administrators would be appointed by the chief judge to serve at his pleasure but would be expected to work closely with the Administrative Office of the Courts and his area-court administrator.

Finally, the superior-court commissioners (subordinate judicial officers considered earlier) would be created by the legislature to relieve the trial-court judges of the routine duties of family-relations matters, law-and-motion proceedings, minor misdemeanors, probate cases, small-claims actions, and most traffic offenses. These officials would be appointed by the chief judge, acting with the consent of the trial-court judges, to serve at his pleasure. No legislation has been introduced to effect this system in California.

## THE NEW YORK MODEL

Unlike the California proposal, the schema recommended for New York rests upon a type-of-court foundation rather than a regional basis. Stated differently, instead of all court-administration duties being performed within each geographical area, such functions are divided among state judicial agencies, each of which controls a different layer of tribunals. However, the proposals for both New York and California emphasize a highly centralized form of judicial administration, where the power to appoint administrators at the intermediate appellate- and trial-court levels is lodged at the top, not with the judges of the court to which the appointment is to be made.

Figure 3-4 depicts a recommended judicial management structure for New York, with administrative organs responsible for different kinds of courts. This figure also requires elaboration in several respects. First, the Chief Judge of the Court of Appeals is the equivalent of the chief justice in other states. He would appoint the Chief Administrative Judge, who during his four-year term would be responsible for the management of the entire statewide court system. This appointee need not be a judge or a state resident (at the time of his selection). He would be empowered to choose four Deputy Chief Administrators—one for Administrative Services, one for Appellate Court and Judicial Services, one for the Trial Courts of the Second Judicial Region (the area outside this metropolis). However, with regard to the latter two officials, he must make his selections from trial-court or intermediate-appellate judges. All of these managers would serve at his pleasure.

Second, these executives would be expected to perform highly diverse functions. The Deputy Chief Administrator for Administrative Services would undertake the coordination of eleven uniform statewide efforts (accounting and budgeting, data processing, facilities management, legal services, management-information services, personnel matters, planning, the settling of court procedures, public-relations work, purchasing, and research) and the coordination of seven other statewide activities (criminal-justice programs, family-law programs, indigent legal services, lower court plans, mental-health information services, pretrial assistance, and probation). His span of managerial control (the number of agency heads reporting directly to him) is realistic since it numbers only eleven.

**Figure 3–4: Proposed New York Judicial Administration Structure**

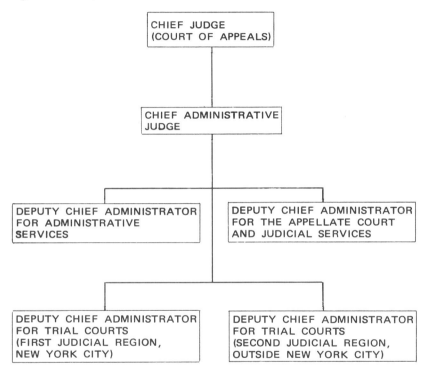

Source: Adapted from . . . *And Justice for All,* 3 vols. (Albany, N.Y.: Temporary Commission on the New York State Court System, 1973), 1:21.

The Deputy Chief Administrator for the Appellate Court and Judicial Services would be the administrative judge for the intermediate appellate court and would be entrusted with the performance of the following duties: the direction of the annual state judicial conferences; the establishment of judicial training programs (including sentencing institutes); supervision of the office of secretary of the committees on alternatives to the judicial disposition of cases; supervision of the law-reporting bureau; and technical assistance to judges. The Deputy Chief Administrator for the First Region would have no specified responsibilities except the appointment of three administrative judges to serve at his pleasure—one for the Superior Court (a trial court with general jurisdiction) of New York City; one for the Civil Court (a lower court) of this city; and one for the Criminal Court (another lower court) of this municipality. These appointees would have diurnal responsibilities for court operations. Finally, the Chief Deputy Administrator for the Second Region would be expected to carry out similar duties. The first and second judicial regions were established upon several bases: the size and diversity of this state, the concentration of people in New York City, a desire to equalize caseloads, and the need to shorten lines of communication.

It is noteworthy that the first two Deputy Chief Administrators, along with the Chief Administrative Judge, represent functional divisions of administrative duties whereas the latter two deputies symbolize a geographical distribution of responsibilities. The appointive powers of the latter two executives represent the only gesture toward decentralization in this proposed system. Bills to implement this system were introduced in the New York legislature in 1973 and are now in effect.

## CONCLUSIONS

This section has furnished a taxonomy of an emerging component of judicial administration: personnel management at the state level. I have examined some salient judicial personnel matters, some major problems affecting court-related employees (supervisory and supportive), and two plans recently suggested for adoption in California and New York. My concluding reflections center on a growing consensus on the subject of court-related employees. This agreement is implicit in the prototypes advocated for both New York and California, and promises to include the following.

1. Court employees at all levels should belong to one state judicial department.

2. The management of personnel within a unified state court system centers on the establishment of procedures for a title structure, job definitions, classification systems, qualifications, appointments, promotions, transfers, leaves of absence, resignations and reinstatement, performance

rating, sick leave, vacations, time allowances, and criteria for removal. 3. Personnel management should emulate the practices followed by the executive and legislative civil services. On this point much discussion centers on whether judicial administrative employees (especially at the trial-court levels) should be incorporated into a state civil service (or personnel system), as in Maryland, or whether a separate judicial civil service (or merit system) should be established, as in New Jersey, Colorado, and Iowa, or proposed, as in Michigan. The trend is clearly toward the establishment of a separate judicial civil service, which would be financed by each state, along with the salaries and fringe benefits accorded to such workers. The Institute of Judicial Administration recently put the case for this system as follows:

A separate judicial personnel system is desirable . . . because it insures that employees of the judicial branch will not be under the control of or subject to the rules and regulations of another coordinate branch of government, thus helping to maintain judicial independence.[19]

However, even if such proposals are enacted, they will probably begin to mirror the state civil services in many respects, especially with regard to the degree of job security and the benefits offered to court employees. 4. A uniform system of position classification and levels of compensation should be established for court employees. The norm ought to approximate equal pay for equal work. However, workload variations may lead to renumerative differences. For instance, in Texas a legislative committee recently suggested the payment of salaries twenty percent higher for urban trial-court judges than for their rural counterparts. 5. These uniformities ought to embrace fringe benefits as well as salaries. A "cafeteria approach," advocated by a nationally known consulting firm (Ernst and Ernst), would allow court employees a range of choices in benefits up to a percentage of their base salary. This idea has already been suggested for adoption in Michigan. The program facilitates the goal of achieving compensational uniformity, since the employees themselves would make the selection of benefits instead of having them imposed from above. 6. A state judicial department should install a system of open and competitive application, examination, and appointment of new employees reflecting the special requirements of each kind of job with respect to education, professional certification, and experience.

7. Judicial employment should be as free as possible of discrimination based on race, age, sex, religion, or political affiliation.

8. Uniform procedures for making regular job-performance evaluations should be formulated.

9. Discipline or discharge of court employees should prevail only for specified causes, in accordance with due process of law.

10. The transfer of individuals from one area within a state to another should be permitted without loss of compensation, seniority, or fringe benefits.

11. As a state shifts to a unified court system, no employee should suffer a diminution of the following kinds of benefits: retirement pay, life insurance, health coverage, accident protection, disability compensation, dental insurance, workmen's compensation, and any gains achieved from lawful collective bargaining.

One expert on judicial administration, Ernest Friesen, Jr., recently predicted that most states would adopt such a public personnel system. However, he and other specialists in this field have been pessimistic about its efficacy, for they view court-related personnel as being caught in a dilemma. If their jobs stem from patronage, court employees tend to be subservient to their sponsors. They tend toward mediocrity because they were hired as a reward for political services rather than for their competence. However, if their jobs are placed within a civil service system, there is the likelihood of rigidity because, quite often, a premium is put on an excessive adherence to rules and the avoidance of trouble. No lateral entry would be permitted. Nor would organizational growth be encouraged. Both alternatives frustrate attempts to improve the effectiveness of judicial administration. Nevertheless, as states contemplate the establishment of a judicial personnel system while seeking to avoid this apparent dilemma, they may start with the advice offered by Pound in 1940:

Organization of the non-judicial administrative business of the courts calls for complete and efficient supervision, under rules of court, which is best to be obtained by unification of the judiciary as a whole, with responsible headship, charged with supervision of the subordinate supervising . . . officers.[20]

# 4

# ANCILLARY DEVELOPMENTS

## MICHIGAN: A CASE STUDY IN UNIFICATION, FINANCING, AND PERSONNEL

When a state reorganizes its judiciary, it tries to provide a system that is competent, fair, uniform, and effective. Such reform embraces at least seven criteria: (1) the establishment of a central judicial policy-making body, such as a judicial council with judges, other lawyers, and the public; a judicial conference with judges and court administrators; or the state supreme court, or a single chief executive, such as the chief justice; (2) the creation of a state judicial administrator to help form and implement court policies; (3) the authorizing of this high state tribunal to make all rules of practice and procedure; (4) the granting of power to the tribunal to assign judges and court-related employees from one jurisdiction to another as needs arise; (5) the provision of state financing of virtually all judicial expenses; (6) the enactment of a court personnel system; and (7) the unification of all lower courts. The states have gradually moved toward achieving these goals. Michigan represents the latest case of staggered conversion. It has moved toward these goals in four uneven phases, which may end in success within the next few years. As a consultant for Ernst and Ernst, which, in December, 1973, completed a thorough investigation of the court system in this state, the author was able to explore the high points in the unfolding of these stages.

## PHASE ONE: 1952-62

The Michigan judicial structure consists of four segments: a state supreme court, a court of appeals, circuit courts, and a slowly shrinking potpourri of lower tribunals (courts of limited or special criminal or civil jurisdiction). This organization embraces 246 courts and at least 5,215 employees.[1] (See Figure 4-1.) The first recognition that the judicial structure needed centralized management came in 1952, when Michigan, along with Virginia, became the fourth jurisdiction to establish a state court administrator's office as a staff arm of the state supreme court.[2] At the time of its creation, the court administrator (appointed by the court to serve at its pleasure) faced several limitations. First, this authority rested only on a statutory basis, not a constitutional foundation. Second, his main task was the collection and promulgation of judicial statistics.[3] Third, he could do little to reduce the chronic civil delay in the trial courts of Wayne and Pontiac counties, which embrace the Detroit area.[4] Nonetheless, this step was a prelude for more extensive changes in the Michigan judiciary.

## PHASE TWO: 1963-70

The second phase of judicial reorganization in Michigan began in 1963, when the voters approved a new constitution—the fourth since 1835—that became operative on January 1, 1964.[5] Its judicial article authorized part of a court-modernization dream by providing for innovations that met three of the seven standards for state judicial reorganizations. First, the state court administrator's office was strengthened by inclusion in the constitution and by a shift of authority to define its functions from the legislature to the supreme court.[6] Second, a central judicial policy-making body was created in the form of the existing supreme court, which was entrusted with selecting one of its members as chief justice; charting his duties; appointing a state judicial administrator, enumerating his responsibilities; choosing other assistants, presumably deputies of this official, regional court executives if desired, and trial-court administrators;[7] and exercising "general superintending control over courts" in this state.[8] This model of judicial supervision is horizontal, since all managerial responsibility rests with a collegial structure of seven justices rather than with one of them (namely, the chief justice). By contrast, other states, such as Colorado and New Jersey, have adopted the latter, a vertical

**Figure 4-1: The Structure of the Michigan Judicial System**

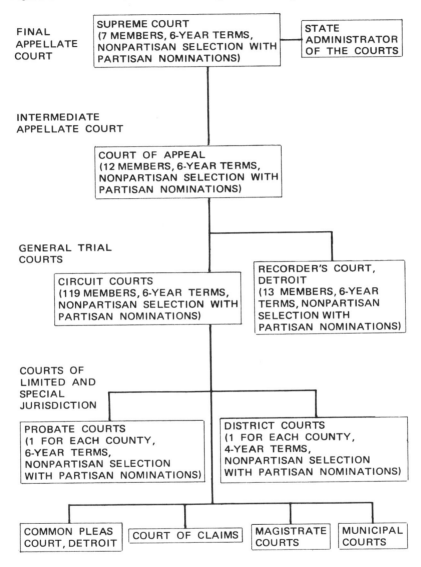

Source: *Michigan Annotated Compiled Laws, Constitutional Articles 4 to End* (St. Paul, Minn.: West Publishing Company, 1967), 2: Art. 6, secs. 1–3, 8, 11, 15–16, 26, along with "Convention Comment" for each section; *Organizational Concepts for a Unified Court System in the State of Michigan* (Detroit, Mich.: Ernst and Ernst, 1973), p. 2.

schema, although in practice a skilled chief justice usually consults with his colleagues.[9] Third, the state supreme court was entrusted with the responsibility for making and promulgating rules of practice and procedure for all subordinate tribunals.[10]

The new constitution also laid the groundwork for attempts to carry out the four remaining standards of judicial reorganization.

First, the "superintending" provision gave the general supreme-court power to assign its judicial and other court-related personnel in whatever directions it deemed appropriate. Another source of such power was the provision that the state "supreme court . . . shall have general supervision of its staff."[11] Since 1968, the highest court in the state has wielded partial authority to transfer general trial- and lower-court judges horizontally but not vertically.[12] The presiding district-court judges may also shift their colleagues to adjoining districts upon request.[13]

Second, the new constitution anticipated state court financing by allowing the highest state court to prepare its own budget for legislative submission and to spend appropriations for its operations as it sees fit.[14] Judges at all levels may be able to extract some funds from local governmental units by issuing writs of mandamus.[15]

Third, the new document contained the seeds of lower-court unification by referring to "one court of justice"[16] with appellate and trial branches scattered throughout the state. Moreover, the legislature may establish lower tribunals only by two-thirds vote of both houses.[17] This provision removed the constitutional basis for tribunals of limited or special jurisdiction and made their abolition considerably easier. At that time, Michigan contained eight kinds of minor courts: justice-of-the-peace, circuit-court commissioners, a common pleas court in Detroit, a court of claims, magistrate courts, municipal courts, probate courts, and a superior court in Grand Rapids. The new charter eliminated the first two courts. The remaining tribunals exist at legislative pleasure with a lone exception, the probate court, which still rests on a constitutional foundation (although the legislature is empowered to change the jurisdictional boundaries of this judicial organization). (See Figure 4-1.) In 1968, the legislature enacted a law providing for a single tier of district courts, which would eventually absorb the jurisdiction of the other lower courts.[18] In April, 1972, the Special Commission to Review Article VI (commonly known as the Michigan Judicial Revision Commission) urged the state legislature to permit the absorption of the probate courts by the circuit tribunals and the elimination of the recorder's and common pleas courts in Detroit, accompanied by a transfer of their functions to the local circuit court.[19]

Finally, the new constitution suggested a basis for the establishment of a state judicial-personnel system by granting the supreme court control of its staff at all levels, especially the power to appoint and remove its employees.[20] Furthermore, the Judicial Revision Commission advocated the expansion of this provision to include the power of the state judicial administrator to establish court-related personnel classifications and qualifications.[21]

PHASE THREE: 1971-73

Although the first three concepts of judicial reorganization (a state court administrator's office, a central judicial policy organ, and one judicial rule-making authority) have taken effect, there has been no success—apart from the district court legislation in 1968—in implementing the four remaining standards of central assignment powers (although the circuit courts exercise such oversight over the minor courts within their jurisdiction); state financing of all judicial costs; the achievement of lower-court unification; and the creation of a statewide court-employees system. During the last few years, signs of ferment in these areas have become apparent.

First, in April, 1973, Representative Bill Huffman introduced legislation (now pending in the House Appropriations Committee) providing for two kinds of assignment powers. One would empower the supreme court or its court administrator to make horizontal transfers of circuit, probate, and district-court judges. The other would enable presiding district-court judges to shift members of their bench temporarily to another district upon request.

Second, a few months earlier, the chief justice of the supreme court, Thomas M. Kavanagh, asked the legislature to enact full state court financing. The form of his request was unusual. Instead of seeking a unified judicial budget subject to legislative (but not executive) review, he endorsed an apparently unprecedented idea—a constitutionally guaranteed 3 percent of the annual state budget (or $141 million for 1973). Since no state has granted its judiciary more than 2 percent of its annual (or biennial) budget, and since only nine states have devoted more than 1 percent for this purpose, his proposal died stillborn. Even the support of his prestigious colleagues, who include two former governors (G. Mennen

Williams and John Swainson), will probably fail to resurrect this idea. Huffman's legislation also contained a more modest proposal: an incremental approach to the full state financing of all district-court expenses by January 1, 1974. These costs would embrace all operating and capital (or maintenance) items. All funds raised by these courts would belong to the state's general fund. The forty-five counties in Michigan would keep revenues deriving from fines for violations of the state penal code as well as fines and court costs for infringements of local ordinances.

Third, the matter of lower-court unification (principally affecting Wayne County) received attention during that spring. Both houses of the legislature witnessed the introduction of legislation to abolish the remaining twenty-eight municipal courts by January 1, 1975. Furthermore, the court administrator's office recommended the abolition of another lower court: the common pleas court in Detroit. The functions of both minor courts would devolve to the nearest district court.

Fourth, the Huffman bill proposed a step toward incorporating judicial employees into a personnel system by empowering the state court administrator (formerly William Hart, now Einar Bolin) to establish position classifications and minimum qualifications for district-court employees. Such personnel would be eligible to join the State Employees Retirement System. This provision does not prevent the creation of a separate judicial-personnel department. Moreover, the court administrator's power is partially offset by what amounts to a "grandfather" clause that both changes must forbid a diminution of seniority rights, annual leave, sick leave, longevity pay, and retirement benefits for employees of any courts abolished under judicial unification.

The last proposed clause of the Huffman bill echoes a recommendation made two years earlier in consultant Norman Paelke's exhaustive study of judicial personnel in Michigan. In that analysis, he put forth other noteworthy recommendations. For instance, he suggested three considerations that influence the classifications and salaries of judicial employees: the local government unit to which the court is attached, the existence of a personnel system, and the presence of a union or association. Furthermore, he urged that all county and city employees performing a trial-court function (as well as all trial-court employees) should be included in a state judicial-personnel system. These employees include the county clerks and staff, friends of the court, adult-probation officers, and sheriffs' deputies and local policemen. Moreover, he suggested that the state would have to set up a 10-percent pay differential for court personnel within the same position classifications becuase of geographical variations in living costs.[22]

PHASE FOUR: LATE 1973-74

Although none of the legislation proposed in early 1973 has passed so far, ferment toward judicial modernization in Michigan continues. Illustrative of this process were the introduction of a bill in the lower house to eliminate the remaining municipal courts by 1977 and two suggestions by Governor William G. Milliken—the need for the legislature to move toward full state judicial financing by assuming the estimated $16 million current operating costs for all minor courts and the desirability of a constitutional amendment that would establish a new mode of judicial selection, the Missouri plan, with its nominating commission, appointments by the governor from names on the commission list, and an opportunity to seek another term by running without opposition.

At the same time the thrust toward judicial reorganization mounted when the state court administrator's office received a grant from the Law Enforcement Assistance Administration in 1973 and accepted a competitive bid from the nationally respected consulting firm of Ernst and Ernst to investigate how the remaining standards of court reform —the assignment, financing, unification, and personnel aspects—might be achieved. Parenthetically, the study also covered two highly technical areas: the development of a five-year plan to facilitate statewide planning and administration by the supreme-court systems department and the judicial data center (two branches of the state court administrator's office) and the design and installation of a cost-allocation and charging system for this center.

A series of reports completed by Ernst and Ernst in December, 1973, contained a spate of general and detailed suggestions for implementing the remaining criteria of judicial modernization. Among the cardinal recommendations were the following.

1. Although no changes in the present judicial-assignment powers of the state supreme court and the various presiding trial-court judges were prescribed, the assignment of other court-related personnel was entrusted to a set of regional court administrators, whose functions will be described shortly.

2. The state financing of all judicial levels was endorsed but has still not been authorized by the legislature.

3. The court-unification proposals merit extensive attention because of their scope. The highest state tribunal was asked to establish a regional administrative structure for overseeing the work of the other courts. This paradigm would consist of regional superintending judges, regional

court administrators, and assistants to the latter if the caseloads warrant. (See Figure 4-2.) Parallel lines of authority would exist as judicial matters travel from trial-court presiding judges through regional superintending judges to the chief justice and as administrative problems arise from local court administrators through the regional

**Figure 4-2: Proposed Judicial Structure for Michigan, a Simplified Version**

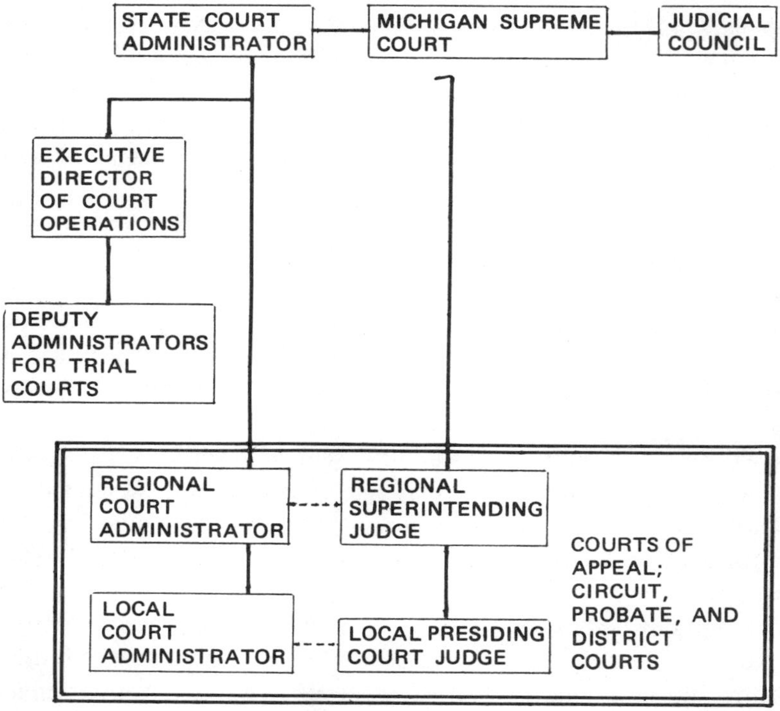

Legend:
```
_____  =  Reporting Relationships
- - - - -  =  Functional Relationships
========  =  Intermediate Appellate and Trial Courts
```

Source: Adapted from *Organizational Concepts for a Unified Court System in the State of Michigan* (Detroit, Mich.: Ernst and Ernst, 1973), pp. 53, 62, 72-74.

court administrator to the state court administrator. These reporting patterns would follow what is commonly labeled the "hospital" model derived from oragnizational relationships between doctors and adminis-trators and popularized recently by Warren E. Burger, the Chief Justice of the United States Supreme Court.

Moreover, this structure emulates the centralized judicial models established in such states as New Jersey and Colorado and proposed in California and New York. In contrast, a collegial model, as in Illinois, leaves the appointment of administrative officials not to the state supreme court but to the courts where they will serve. Consequently, the ability of the highest tribunal to carry out uniform, statewide policies is jeopardized. The regional proposal is likely to work in Michigan, not only because it follows the practices of New Jersey and Colorado, but also because it sets up a fairly small span of managerial control: fifteen to eighteen regional judges and administrators reporting directly to their superiors.

Supplementing this model is a recommendation for the establishment of a judicial council in an advisory capacity. Among its members would be the chief justice as chairman, regional superintending judges, one judge from each type of court, the President of the Michigan Bar Association, the chairmen of the Michigan house and senate judiciary committees, the state attorney general, the chief official of the state department of corrections, a defense attorney or public defender, and laymen selected by the governor. The chief justice would be entrusted with appointing regional superintending judges with the advice of the state court administrator, also chosen by him, and the consent of the other justices. Their terms would coincide with the chief justice's. The regional judges would be selected from members of the various trial courts in each region. Such judges would perform administrative as well as judicial duties. Their managerial responsibilities would include the recommendation of regional policies to the chief justice and the implementation of these policies if approved.

Such proposed functions raise at least two questions. One centers upon whether judicial and administrative duties are separable in practice and, as a corollary, whether persistently sharp clashes between regional superintending judges and the regional court administrators are inevitable. The Institute of Judicial Administration[23] and the Temporary Commission on the New York State Court System anticipated such disputes. The other query focuses on whether the concentration of both functions in a single position may prove too much for such judges to handle effectively. On this score the Temporary Commission is skeptical.[24] In Michigan, as in other states, operational experience will provide the best way of answering these questions.

The regional administrators would be chosen by the state court administrator after consultation with the regional superintending judge and after securing the chief justice's approval. Their tenure would be indefinite, since it rests on merit. Regional administrators would be selected from a list of applicants certified by the state court administrator as qualified. Such officials would help the regional superintending judges in carrying out managerial responsibilities. In addition, the regional administrators would implement the rules and orders of the superintending judges if regional in scope, supervise staff members, maintain judicial statistics and records, and oversee the work of local-court administrative personnel.

4. The personnel recommendations also require much discussion because of their breadth. States may choose between inserting their court-related personnel (other than judges) into an existing civil service system or forming a new apparatus. The latter is the trend because it features supreme-court control over personnel and uniform policy applications, because the low partisanship of judiciaries tends to obviate a civil service system, and because this idea supports the most recent thinking in public-personnel administration. A new organization would be designed to avoid the rigidity of state civil service systems while showing concern for job security of its employees.

A Personnel Services Department would be established in the state court administrator's office and would be charged with determining wage levels and fringe benefits, salary structure, negotiation of union contracts, performance evaluation, and research.

A Personnel Advisory Board would be created for handling disciplinary cases and making recommendations to the chief justice, who would be expected to follow them except for compelling reasons. Five board members would be chosen annually—two by the court employees, two by the chief justice, and one member by the other four, to promote fairness.

Also suggested was a fringe-benefits system incorporating all court-related employees into the state supreme court's plan for its justices and employees, the most generous one now in effect. This recommendation signaled an abandonment of the imaginative "cafeteria plan" proposed by Charles Barkdull, a veteran executive for Ernst and Ernst, which would have permitted court-related personnel to choose benefits from a proffered list up to 10 to 15 percent of their annual base salaries. In this way, such benefit levels would be made uniform for such employees throughout the state. However, the supreme court's plan was chosen because it was easier to carry out, despite its narrower degree of choice in benefits.

These proposals (except for the fiscal ones) are expected to be effected soon by the Michigan Supreme Court through its rules. The recommendations will then have to be modified as they are tested for an estimated two or three years. Experimentation of this sort is necessary to avoid freezing unwise administrative policies into law and incurring the displeasure of lawmakers who believe that, by granting the state supreme court broad fiscal and personnel authority through pending legislation, further action on this subject is undesirable until a foundation of operational experience is built.

## A FINAL COMMENT

These recommended changes promise to move Michigan closer to the ideal of a judicial system which is highly competent, equitable, even-handed, and efficient. Unfortunately, a recent survey conducted by the Law Enforcement Assistance Administration in four states (California, Michigan, New Jersey, and Texas) shows that criminal justice personnel and litigants expect outstanding judicial performance but are uncertain about receiving it.[25] Nonetheless, the direction and intensity of this ferment—the spate of changes and proposals—implies that, within the next few years, Michigan will join a growing number of states which are becoming staggered cases of conversion to judicial modernization.

## MODERNIZED COURTS AND THE LOCATION OF PROBATION SERVICES*

*The question of where probation should be placed in the framework of [state] government becomes more critical as its use expands and staff numbers increase. It is time to take a serious look at where probation could function most effectively, rather than using chance and history to support the status quo.*[26]

This comment, from the National Advisory Commission on Criminal Justice Standards and Goals in 1973, centers upon an increasingly salient issue at the intersection between the fields of probation and judicial administration: whether or not state trial-courts should control probation officers performing judicial functions. Since state court reorganization, as well as the unification of state correctional services, is a recent, ongoing phenomenon, this issue has only recently begun to receive scholarly attention.

_____

*Written jointly with Edward S. Piggins, Jr.

But as state courts continue to gain the constitutional and legislative authority to define and regulate their personnel, this question will become highly significant. This research centers upon three facets of the probation-services question: a national perspective; the latest, illustrative case study (Michigan); and a prognosis.

## A NATIONAL PERSPECTIVE

Consideration of the location issue from a national perspective starts with a brief classification of probationary functions. Some duties are non-judicial, such as the gathering and analysis of statistical data, budgetary preparation, and the evaluation of job performance. But most responsibilities are judicial, including presentencing investigations; recommendations for prosecutors (mostly in plea bargaining) and judges about the advisability of release on recognizance; and the supervision of people awaiting or serving sentences without imprisonment.

In a national context the location question is an aspect of a larger matter: whether probation services should be administered by the state or by local units of government. As states assume responsibility for these functions as well as for the management of courts at all levels, they must decide whether to place such tasks within the judicial system, the executive branch, or both sectors. Although a canvass of the professional literature yields little information on this subject, there is enough to discern four schools of thought concerning the resolution of this issue and to order these views along a continuum.[27]

The first viewpoint holds that probation should be included within the judicial branch as part of a unified state court system run by a judicial council (made up of appellate and trial judges, legislators, bar-association representatives, and the public) or by the highest state court. Numerous arguments are cited to support this position. They include the intimate link between probation duties and judging; the desire to make probation officers more responsive to court direction; the necessity of efforts by state judicial departments to increase their autonomy from state and local governmental units through the absorption of as many court-related functionaries as possible; deeper judicial trust in staff members, resulting in greater feedback; higher court awareness of probation difficulties, leading to more judicial assistance; an increased use of pretrial diversion of cases as courts permit greater discretion by their probation staffs; and a stronger willingness to accept the views of such personnel. Furthermore, in reorganizing their courts, at least five states have opted for this choice: New Jersey,[28] New York,[29] Colorado,[30] Louisiana,[31] and New Hampshire.[32] This course of action implements the recommendations of the American Bar Association,[33] the National Commission on the Causes and Prevention of Violence,[34] and the National Conference on the Judiciary,[35] all of whom may be predisposed to favor judicial systems in their clashes with other governmental organizations.

A second school of thought opposes such inclusion but shows indifference to the local alternatives for probation services. Several arguments underlie this position: a lack of judicial time, outlook, competence, and training for such a role; a tendency of officers to give higher priority to court services rather than probationers; an inclination of courts to require the performance of tasks unrelated to this work, such as errands for judges, serving subpenas, and issuing summons; and subservience to the courts, resulting in a decline in the quality of recommendations. No prominent organization identifies with this position.

A third viewpoint favors a split in probation functions between the executive and judicial sectors. The proposed cleavage centers on the location of postsentencing responsibilities. Recently, the Temporary Commission on the New York State Court System examined this possibility but dismissed it with the following comment:

Of [all] probation functions . . . post-sentence supervision is least related to the courts, and the suggestion to sever this function and place it within the executive [department of state government] has strong initial appeal. However, this would fragment the probation agencies, thereby weakening them, and would limit the flexibility inherent in having one staff perform both [executive and judicial] functions.[36]

A fourth outlook urges the incorporation of probation functions within the executive branch as an agency or as a subdivision of the state corrections department, although the former is preferred. Numerous contentions are advanced to support this position: a probable improvement in the coordination of all correctional work; better planning and cooperation with state educational, employment, housing, medical, and rehabilitative servcies; the likelihood of more rational decisions on the best allocation of resources; a stronger budgetary role, since judges would no longer present and negotiate probation requests with executive-branch officials; and an end to a conflict of interest stemming from courts reviewing their own probation practices.[37] The leading proponents of this school are the

Wickersham Commission,[38] the American Correctional Association,[39] the National Council on Crime and Delinquency,[40] the President's Commission on Law Enforcement and the Administration of Justice,[41] the National Advisory Commission on Criminal Justice Standards and Goals,[42] and the noted Wisconsin Citizens Study Committee on Judicial Organization.[43] This viewpoint has gained currency partly because its advocacy extends well beyond the correctional field.

## THE CASE OF MICHIGAN

Michigan is the latest illustration of a state facing the location issue. A prominent consulting firm, Ernst and Ernst, illuminated this matter by commenting:

[An] important concern, particularly if the Michigan courts are to be organized into a single organization, will be the decision as to what local personnel are to be considered part of the Judicial System. For example, are Sheriff's Deputies, Bailiffs, Corrections Officers, and the like, a part of the Court, or will they be left as local government employees? The decision will have an important bearing on the organization, and also the court system financing.[44]

In Michigan the location of probation services is technically within the executive branch of the state government. The Michigan Corrections Commission may appoint and remove probation officers,[45] who receive supervision from the Assistant Director of Corrections.[46]

However, this placement is blurred by three statutes. First, the judges of the local courts are empowered to recommend the appointment of probation officers to the Commission.[47] Second, the Commission "shall remove such . . . officers appointed by it upon the recommendation of the judge or judges of courts of cities having a population in excess of 250,000 . . . upon . . . the filing"[48] . . . of a certificate that the officer has been accorded a hearing and has been found incompetent, guilty of misconduct, negligent, or insubordinate. Presumably in areas with fewer than 250,000 people, the Commission holds an option in this matter. Third, the salaries of such employees come from the counties in which they work.[49] Consequently, the judiciary and the county commissions exercise substantial, if not decisive, power over the day-to-day operations of probation officers despite their formal location.

In December, 1973, Ernst and Ernst completed a report urging the exclusive control (rather than the present sharing) of probation functions by the district courts that now provide these services.[50] However, the study also recommended that, after a few years, the state supreme court, operating through its administrative office, should reevaluate this decision when an experiential base has been formed. The recommendation for a continued judicial role in probation control derived from a unique four-point test devised by Eugene W. Kuthy, a high-ranking executive for this consulting firm:

1. Does a specifically defined district court functioning *directly* and *materially* effect the expeditious, consistent and equitable adjudication of cases and controversies properly within its jurisdiction?
2. If the answer is yes, then this function should be under the exclusive control of the district [court]. If the answer is no, then this function should be further tested by the following questions:
   a. Are there any other compelling administrative reasons for retaining this function under the exclusive control of the district court?
   b. Are there any statutes that compel retention of this function under the exclusive control of the district court? (This test would not preclude recommendations for statutory changes, if appropriate).
3. If the answer is yes, then this function should be under the exclusive control of the district court. If the answer is no, then this function should be further tested by the following question: Is there another state or local governmental agency that could more effectively or more appropriately perform this function?
4. If the answer is yes, then this function should be examined to determine the advantages and disadvantages of assigning the function to another local or state agency.[51]

This procedure warrants at least three comments. First, the advocacy of judicial inclusion of probation-control functions stemmed from affirmative responses to questions 1 and 2b. Second, it is possible that, after two or three years of operational experience, district courts may come to favor a removal of probation services from their control (items 3 and 4). An answer is probable within that time, since the state court administrator's office intends to conduct periodic evaluations of the judicial system. Third, although the report centered only on an examination of the district courts, this test extends to all other lower courts as well as the general trial courts in this state. (See Figure 4-1.) But such applications may be deferred because of legislative opposition which may be overcome only by compelling evidence that an inclusion policy does not work.

At the general trial-court level, the implications of probational location are significant. One salient illustration is the recorder's court in Detroit, the largest trial court in the state.

The charter of 1857 creating the recorder's court gave it the same jurisdiction as the old mayor's court, whose powers and duties it assumed. Furthermore, it was granted the criminal jurisdiction which, before that time, had been vested in the Circuit Court of Wayne County. By enactment of the Michigan legislature in 1919, the recorder's court was given exclusive jurisdiction of all criminal cases, both felonies and misdemeanors, arising within the corporate limits of Detroit. In addition, this court was granted concurrent jurisdiction in civil cases with the Circuit Court of Wayne County, that is, in transitory actions where one or both parties have been residents of Detroit.

The Probation Department in the recorder's court is subject to the laws of this state. The earliest law, passed in 1903, was very brief and did little more than establish the principle that the probation officer is both a confidential advisor of the court and subject to state supervision. This idea is still in the law.

In 1913, the Michigan legislature afforded substantial meaning to this principle by greatly enlarging the authority and responsibility of probation officers. It also gave complete discretion to the courts, including the recorder's court, to determine whether an offender was suitable for probation. Such treatment was no longer restricted to first offenders; instead, it was entirely within the power of the court, supplemented with such advice as the court might require from the probation officer.[52] This enlargement of the court's discretion is an indication that the legislature was satisfied with the care that judges had exercised in the use of probation. It is also significant because it denotes legislative approval of the judges' use of probation. Moreover, these acts tend to confirm the original intent of the state legislature to vest exclusive control of probationary functions in the judiciary.

For many years the recorder's court probation department has functioned successfully under the sole direction of the judges in this court and the Wayne County Civil Service Commission. With the recent addition of twenty-two new state parole officers employed by the Michigan Corrections Commission, there will probably be efforts to include other personnel, such as probation officers, wholly within the executive domain of state government.[53]

As mentioned earlier, numerous advantages and disadvantages accrue from the placement of probation services in the judicial or executive sectors. However, extensive personal experience in the recorder's court suggests that the overriding responsibilities of the probation officers are judicial. The presentence investigation is the cardinal example. Other illustrations encompass an advisory function to judges and the supervision of offenders who are awaiting or serving sentences without imprisonment. In addition, each of the present twenty recorder's court judges has been assigned a probation officer, who serves as an aide and performs numerous court-related functions. Consequently, duty-related advantages result from the inclusion of probation within the judicial branch as part of a unified state court system.

Nonetheless, some drawbacks to such inclusion are evident. First, many judges do not have enough time to become aware of the needs of probation services, nor do they have the training to perform such a role. Second, probation officers frequently confront a spate of tasks unrelated to their work, such as verifying records, assisting judges with their correspondence, and, in some cases, running errands. In general, however, personal experience within the recorder's court confirms that far more benefits result from judicial inclusion.

The recent assignment of new probation officers to this court by the state corrections commission is apparently the first attempt to insert such services wholly within the executive branch. Several putative benefits have been advanced. First, it is expected that coordination with other correctional agencies in the state would improve, especially as lines of authority are clarified and as communication and cooperation increase. Second, the judges of the recorder's court would be relieved of an additional burden—solving the probational problems of the court. Third, it is possible that such inclusion may raise the effectiveness of probation officers in working with the educational, employment, and rehabilitative services in Michigan.

The alleged shortcomings of such a placement approach have been suggested earlier: the several statutes empowering the judges of various trial courts to recommend the appointment and removal of probation officers as well as the payment of probation officers in the recorder's court by Wayne County. Furthermore, a shift of probation services from judicial to executive control would probably face much resistance, not only from judges but also from probation employees, if only because such a change entails an uprooting of habitual work relationships.

## RESOLVING THE PROBATION-SERVICES LOCATION ISSUE

A prognosis about the resolution of the location issue in Michigan is feasible. However, which governmental unit should control probation cannot be answered merely by selecting one of the four solutions mentioned earlier. No one governmental unit, as presently constituted, can simultaneously carry out the needs of both the probationer and society, regardless of whether the organization is judicial or executive. When a person or group commits a crime within the territorial boundaries of a court, that court must invoke jurisdiction for trial, release, or conviction and sentencing. In this sense, courts must regulate convicted persons in order to discharge their constitutional obligations. Since probation officers are clearly involved in this regulatory task and have amassed considerable expertise, it may be advisable for them to be placed wholly within the judicial domain. But the most likely resolution of this issue is suggested by the National Advisory Commission on Criminal Justice Standards and Goals:

. . . in view of the current variety of local arrangements, it may for the present be appropriate for personnel carrying out services to the courts to be employed by the probation division of a unified state corrections system but detailed to perform court services.[54]

# 5

# CONCLUSION

What is the future of state court management? The preceding sections of this study make an answer evident: state court management is proceeding toward the attainment of unified state judicial systems modeled after Pound's ideal. Such unification embraces broad rule-making authority by the highest state court over all subordinate tribunals, extensive powers to assign judges and court-related personnel in all directions within the state judicial department, the advent of total state court financing, and the emergence of state judicial personnel systems. This change also encompasses the placement of ultimate administrative responsibility upon a single official, usually the chief justice. Furthermore, state court unification necessitates the establishment of a single layer of lower courts with uniform jurisdiction, a development that may be fully successful within the next ten to fifteen years. Additionally, it embraces the creation of a single highest state appeals court for criminal and civil matters.

The unification movement has numerous implications for state courts. One is that, for the first time, the tribunals will no longer be merely a collection of semi-autonomous entities, or fiefdoms, but will become a genuine system resembling corporations, with the highest state court as top management setting overall policies and managing by exception, with the intermediate appellate courts serving as a middle-management level, with the chief trial-court judges functioning as supervisors, and with the general and lower trial-court judges, attorneys, and support personnel constituting the rank and file of the system.

A second implication is that a unified state judiciary, although a system in itself, will better serve as a component within the far larger justice system. Speaking with one voice will enhance the judiciary's ability to coordinate and plan judicial efforts with those of the police and correctional agencies on a statewide basis. The state judicial department will constitute the intermediate part of a funnel, with the police at its mouth

**Figure 5-1: A Unified Justice System**

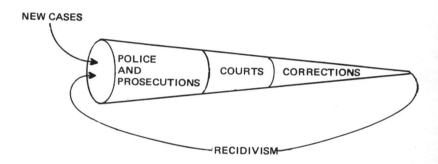

and the correctional organizations near its apex. Together, these segments may be able to reach a consensus on the advisability of decriminalizing some areas of human conduct (especially crimes without victims) and devote their efforts toward cases regarded as more important. They will be able to combine their efforts in many other respects, since they are interdependent and the policies of one component lead to important repercussions in the other segments. In short, judicial unification, vertical change, is a prerequisite for the formation of an overall justice system and for criminal-justice unification, horizontal change.

A third implication is that court unification is a *sine qua non* for reducing the necessity of plea bargaining. Under a unified court structure, personnel, money, and time will be planned and allocated optimally, so that jury trials (civil as well as criminal) will no longer clog judicial calendars and force defendants to give up their right to trial, prosecutors to bargain away strong cases in the name of expediency and acceleration in the flow of court business.

A fourth implication is that some judicial functions will be centralized. Trial-court judges will probably encounter more restrictions on their sentencing power. These limitations will come from the highest state court, acting through its judicial administrator, whose staff will be investigating and recommending ways of making such decision making as uniform as possible throughout the state. These changes may prevail even if state legislatures still permit considerable sentencing discretion, for the state court administrators will be forming and enforcing a set of policies within the statutory guidelines. They may impose a heavy burden on judges to defend exceptions to these rules (which may represent the products of a statewide sentencing council made up of judges at different levels of the system). Nonetheless, since cases are unique, though similar, a residue of latitude will probably remain. Indeed, such prestigious bodies as the President's Commission on Law Enforcement and the Administration of Justice (1967), the American Bar Association (1968), and the National Advisory Commission on Criminal Justice Standards and Goals (1973) have urged the retention of such flexibility.

A fifth implication is that, despite centralization and standardization, geographical distances as well as the need for the wholehearted cooperation of trial judges will probably compel top management to share much of its authority with its subordinates. Centralization will have been largely a prelude to decentralization. Instead of an authoritarian model, it is more likely that the newly revamped state court systems will rely on a collegial model, as many universities and human relations-oriented organizations have done. The collective determination of court goals and methods of attaining them is probable as such decision-making patterns as management by objectives spread from other governmental organizations to the judiciary.

A sixth implication is that a concomitant of state judicial unification is the statewide financing of all courts. Although the two concepts are inextricably linked, the latter required separation to expedite analysis. But without such fiscal change, judicial consolidation remains largely a paper reform. In many states that now share the payment of judicial costs with local governmental units, it will be necessary to move in one of two directions: to extend state financial responsibility on the basis of kinds of expenses or on the level of the judicial organizations (such as trial courts of general or limited jurisdiction). Within the next decade most, if not all, states will probably have adopted such financing. This financing is likely to be phased in over a period of several years.

A seventh implication is that state court unfication entails judicial control over its own personnel. Like financing, the personnel matter is interwoven with the idea of consolidation and makes a separation artificial, even though necessary. In the main, the highest state courts will be setting up judicial civil services to embrace all support employees, regardless of the rank or location within the system. The term "support employees" will also be extended to include all services (such as courthouse security) that courts rely upon other governmental agencies to provide. Like financing, this change will make trial courts more nearly equal in their integrity, competence, and effectiveness. Furthermore, improving the quality of court-related personnel generates pressure to improve the abilities of judges through such long-espoused concepts as the Missouri plan of selection and its extension to all judicial echelons.

This enumeration of implications by no means exhausts the possibilities. This list merely illustrates some of the notable ripples likely to be created by the advent of state court unification. It demonstrates that such a change is really a master stroke that makes the other dominoes, including financing and personnel, fall. Moreover, it is a concept that will soon have to be enacted in the remaining states to alleviate public discontent with the courts and to move a significant distance towards tribunals that are honest, competent, evenhanded, and effective. Nonetheless, the unfinished task of state judicial modernization remains substantial. In 1973, the National Advisory Commission on Criminal Justice Standards and Goals summarized this prospect in the following words:

> The court system in the United States is in serious difficulty. There are too many defendants for the existing system to handle effectively and efficiently. Backlogs are enormous; workloads are increasing. The entire court system is underfinanced . . .
>
> The crisis in the courts has not escaped the attention of the general public. Critical discussions of the court processing of defendants have appeared in the news media with distressing frequency. Citizens—as victims, witnesses, defendants, or jurors—experience delay, inconvenience, and confusion. These personal experiences contribute to an undercurrent of popular dissatisfaction that is undermining the public's respect for the American court system.[1]

# NOTES AND SOURCES

## FOREWORD

1.  National Advisory Commission on Criminal Justice Standards and Goals, *Courts* (Washington, D.C.: U.S. Government Printing Office, 1973), pp. 171-77.
2.  Norval Morris, "The Law Is a Busybody," *New York Times Magazine,* April 1, 1973, pp. 10-11, 58-62.

## 1. PROGRESS IN STATE COURT UNIFICATION

1.  Roscoe Pound, "Principles and Outline of a Modern Unified Court System," *Journal of the American Judicature Society* 23 (April 1940): 233.
2.  Roscoe Pound, "The Causes of Popular Dissatisfaction with the Administration of Justice," *Journal of the American Judicature Society* 46 (August 1962): 62-63.
3.  Roscoe Pound, "Organization of Courts," *Journal of the American Judicature Society* 11 (October 1927): 78, 81-82.
4.  Advisory Commission on Intergovernmental Relations, *State-Local Relations in the Criminal Justice System* (Washington, D.C.: U.S. Government Printing Office, 1971), p. 191.
5.  Colorado, *Constitution* (1876), art. 6 (1962), sec. 5 (3-4), 1966.
6.  Fannie J. Klein et al., *Judicial Administration—1971-1972* (New York: The Institute of Judicial Administration, 1972), p. 735.
7.  E. C. Friesen, Jr. et al., *Report on the Management of the Ventura County Courts,* 3 vols. (Denver, Colo.: The Institute for Court Management, 1972), 1: ii-vii.
8.  Robert H. Hall, "President's Page," *Judicature* 56 (April 1973): 356.
9.  R. Stanley Lowe, "Unified Courts in America: The Legacy of Roscoe Pound," *Judicature* 56 (March 1973): 323.
10.  *1971 Annual Report to the Supreme Court of Illinois* (Springfield, Ill.: Administrative Office of the Illinois Courts, 1972), pp. 7, 9-10.
11.  Glenn Winters, "The Case for a Two-Level State Court System," *Judicature* 50 (February 1967): 185-87.
12.  National Commission on Law Observance and Enforcement, *Report on Prosecution* (Washington, D.C.: U.S. Government Printing Office, 1931), pp. 120-121, 158-159, 172-173, 181.

81

13.   American Bar Association, "ABA Model State Judicial Article (1962)," as reprinted in *Task Force Report: The Courts* (Washington, D.C.: U.S. Government Printing Office, 1967), pp. 92-96.
14.   "Text of the Model State Judicial Article," *Journal of the American Judicature Society* 47 (June 1963): 8-12.
15.   National Municipal League, *Modern State Constitution*, 6th ed. rev. (New York: The National Municipal League, 1968), p. 81.
16.   The President's Commission on Law Enforcement and the Administration of Justice, *The Challenge of Crime in a Free Society* (New York: Avon Books, 1968), p. 321.
17.   *Report of the National Advisory Commission on Civil Disorders* (New York: Bantam Books, 1968), pp. 337-38.
18.   *Justice in the States* (Washington, D.C.: Law Enforcement Assistance Administration, 1971), pp. 265-66.
19.   Advisory Commission on Intergovernmental Relations, *For a More Perfect Union—Court Reform* (Washington, D.C.: U.S. Government Printing Office, 1971), pp. 1, 5, 7, 13.
20.   *Reducing Crime and Assuring Justice* (New York: Committee for Economic Development, 1972), pp. 21-22.
21.   National Advisory Commission on Criminal Justice Standards and Goals, *Courts* (Washington, D.C.: U.S. Government Printing Office, 1973), pp. 164-66.
22.   *State-Local Relations* . . . op. cit., pp. 191, 193-194.
23.   Lowe, op. cit., p. 318.
24.   *The Rhode Island Courts* (New York: The Institute of Judicial Administration, 1967), pp. 26, 33, 38, 42.
25.   *Survey of the Judicial System of Maryland* (New York: The Institute of Judicial Administration, 1967), pp. 5, 24-27, 49, 68-69.
26.   *The Judicial System of South Carolina* (New York: The Institute of Judicial Administration, 1971), pp. 97, 102-104, 106-107.
27.   *The Judicial System of Tennessee* (New York: The Institute of Judicial Administration, 1971), pp. 70, 82-83, 88-89.
28.   Letter dated November 19, 1973, from Mrs. Jean Coonrod, Secretary to Chief Justice Glenn Parker, Supreme Court of Wyoming, Cheyenne, Wyoming, 82001.
29.   *From the State Capitals,* Bethune-Jones, Asbury Park, N.J.: March 19, 1973 (pp. 1-2); April 16, 1973 (pp. 1-2).
30.   Ibid., April 30, 1973, p. 3, and May 21, 1973, pp. 2-3.
31.   . . . *And Justice For All,* 3 vols. (Albany, N.Y.: Temporary Commission on the New York State Court System, 1973), 2:8.
32.   *From the State Capitals,* December 3, 1973 (p. 5).
33.   Alan V. Sokolow, "The State of the Judiciary," in *The Book of the States, 1972-1973,* ed. Robert H. Weber (Lexington, Ky.: The Council of State Governments, 1972), 19:120.
34.   Robert A. Martin, "Alabama [Legislature] Approves Judicial Article, Pay Raises, in Eleventh-Hour Vote," *Judicature* 57 (November 1973): 173.
35.   *From the State Capitals,* op. cit., February 26, 1973 (1-2).
36.   Nebraska Legislative Bill 1032 (March 30, 1972), secs. 1-2.
37.   Fannie J. Klein and Ruth J. Witztum, *Judicial Administration—1972-1973* (New York: The Institute of Judicial Administration, 1973), pp. 731-32; *Iowa House File 585,* 65th General Assembly, July 1, 1973, p. i.
38.   *California Unified Trial Court Feasibility Study* (San Francisco: Booz, Allen, and Hamilton, 1971), pp. 48, 50, 60; *California Lower Court Study* (San Francisco: Booz, Allen, and Hamilton, 1971), pp. 49-50.
39.   *Select Committee on Trial Court Delay, Report 4: Unified Trial Court System, Calendar Management* (San Francisco: Select Committee on Trial Court Delay, 1971), pp. 14, 20.

40.   *The Judicial System of Tennessee,* op. cit., pp. 70, 89.
41.   Richard Morehead, "Briscoe, Labor Blamed," *Dallas Morning News,* August 1, 1974; Stewart Davis, "Proposed Constitutional Amendment Soundly Rejected by Voters," *Dallas Morning News,* November 6, 1975.
42.   "Orleans Area Carries Note," *Baton Rouge Advocate,* April 22, 1974.
43.   *Report of the Committee on Court Structure* (Providence, R.I.: Office of the Rhode Island Court Administrator, 1972), pp. 2–3.
44.   Letter dated November 21, 1973, from George Stragalas III, Judicial Administrator, Administrative Office of the Courts, Supreme Court of Arizona, Phoenix, Arizona, 85007.
45.   Kansas House Concurrent Resolution 1018 (1973), sec. 1.
46.   Richard Wilson, "Judicial Amendment Leaves Questions," *Louisville Courier-Journal,* November 6, 1975.
47.   "Michigan Shows Progress in Judicial Reform Efforts," *Detroit Free Press,* January 22, 1974.
48.   *A District Court for New Hampshire* (New York: The Institute of Judicial Administration, 1973), p. 29.
49.   State of Oregon, *Governor's Commission on Judicial Reform, Report No. 1* (Salem, Oreg.: State of Oregon, 1973), p. 1.
50.   Letter dated November 23, 1973, from Robert W. Gibson, Assistant Court Administrator, Office of the Court Administrator, State of Utah, 250 East Broadway, Suite 240, Salt Lake City, Utah, 84111.
51.   Washington Senate Joint Resolution 113 (February 1, 1973).
52.   Letter dated March 17, 1975, from Hon. Forrest J. Bowman, Director, Administrative Office of the Courts, West Virginia Supreme Court of Appeals, E–404, State Capitol, Charleston, West Virginia, 25305.
53.   *Citizens Study Committee on Judicial Organization* (Madison, Wis.: Citizens Study Committee on Judicial Organization, 1973), pp. 73–74; 1973 Wisconsin Assembly Joint Resolution 5 and Assembly Bill 899 (October 19, 1973), pp. 1–2.
54.   Letter dated December 28, 1973, from Lawrence J. Turgeon, Court Administrator, Office of the Court Administrator, Vermont Supreme Court, Montpelier, Vermont 05612.
55.   Lowe, op. cit., p. 316.
56.   Ward v. Village of Monroeville, Ohio, 409 U.S. 57 (1972).
57.   Francis C. Cady, "Court Modernization: Retrospective, Prospective, and Perspective," *Suffolk University Law Review* 6 (Summer 1972): 836.
58.   Pound, "Principles and Outlines of a Modern Unified Court System," p. 233.
59.   Letter from Amato to the author, dated November 25, 1975, along with pertinent materials; Wilson, "Judicial Amendment" Kentucky *Constitution,* secs. 109 (November 4, 1975), 110, nos. 5–6, 115–16.
60.   Letter from Hutcheson to the author, dated November 20, 1975, along with pertinent materials; Davis, "Proposed Constitutional Amendment"; Sam Kinch, Jr., "New State Charter Defeated Badly in Large Counties," *Dallas Morning News,* November 6, 1975; Carolyn Barta, "Revision Election To Be Issue?" *Dallas Morning News,* November 10, 1975.

## 2. DEVELOPMENTS IN STATE COURT FINANCING

1.   Chief Justice Thomas M. Kavanagh, *State of the Judiciary Message* (Detroit, Mich.: Michigan Supreme Court, Court Administrators' Office, 1973), p. 2.
2.   *A Study of the Louisiana Court System* (New York: The Institute of Judicial Administration, 1972), p. 337.
3.   Geoffrey C. Hazard, Jr., Martin B. McNamara, and Irwin F. Sentilles, III, "Court Finance and Unitary Budgeting," *Yale Law Journal* 81 (June 1972): 1288.

4.   *State and Local Financing of the Courts (Tentative Report)* (New York: The Institute of Judicial Administration, 1969), p. 8.
5.   John F. Burke, "The Inherent Powers of the Courts," *Judicature* 57 (January 1974): 247–48.
6.   National Municipal League, *Modern State Constitution*, 6th ed., rev. (New York: The National Municipal League, 1968), p. 14; The President's Commission on Law Enforcement and the Administration of Justice, *The Challenge of Crime in a Free Society* (New York: Avon Books, 1968), p. 322; *Justice in the States* (Washington, D.C.: Law Enforcement Assistance Administration, 1971), p. 266; Advisory Commission on Intergovernmental Relations, *For a More Perfect Union—Court Reform* (Washington, D.C.: U.S. Government Printing Office, 1971), p. 20; E. C. Friesen, Jr., et al. *Report on the Management of the Ventura County Courts,* 3 vols. (Denver, Colo.: The Institute for Court Management, 1972), 1:55, 60, 65–66; *Reducing Crime and Assuring Justice* (New York: Committee for Economic Development, 1972), p. 21; National Advisory Commission on Criminal Justice and Goals, *Courts* (Washington, D.C.: U.S. Government Printing Office, 1973), pp. 164–65; "Text of the Model State Judicial Article," *Journal of the American Judicature Society* 47 (June 1963): 12.
7.   Ralph N. Kleps, "State Court Modernization in the 1970s," *Judicature* 55 (March 1972): 294–95.
8.   Advisory Committee on Intergovernmental Relations, *State-Local Relations in the Criminal Justice System* (Washington, D.C.: U. S. Government Printing Office, 1971), p. 45.
9.   *California Unified Trial Court Feasibility Study* (San Francisco: Booz, Allen, and Hamilton, 1971), p. 107; *California Lower Court Study,* op. cit., pp. 96–98; Select Committee on Trial-Court Delay, *Report 4: Unified Trial Court System,* Calendar Management (San Francisco: Select Committee on Trial-Court Delay, 1971), p. 23; Friesen, Jr., et. al., op. cit., 1:55, 60, 65–66.
10.   *From the State Capitals,* Bethune-Jones, Asbury Park, N.J.: May 7, 1973 (pp. 1–2).
11.   Kansas Senate Joint Resolution 2 (February 27, 1973), sec. 1, p. 1.
12.   Richard Wilson, "Judicial Amendment Leaves Questions," *Louisville Courier-Journal,* November 6, 1975.
13.   *A Study of the Lousiana Court System,* op. cit., pp. 28–31; *Modernizing Louisiana's Courts of Limited Jurisdiction* (Chicago: American Judicature Society, 1973), p. 113.
14.   "AJS Study Spurs Revision of Massachusetts Court Financing," *Judicature* 57 (January 1974): 267–68.
15.   "Michigan Shows Progress in Judicial Reform Efforts," *Detroit Free Press,* January 22, 1974; Roger Lane, "House OKs State Takeover of District Court Financing," *Detroit Free Press,* May 24, 1974.
16.   Alfonzo A. Narvaez, "Governor in Court Plan, Asks to Appoint Judge," *New York Times,* April 23, 1973, pp. 1, 25; . . . *And Justice for All,* 3 vols. (Albany, N.Y.: Temporary Commission on the New York State Court System, 1973), 1:57, 59.
17.   Letter dated December 13, 1973, from A. Evans Kephart, Court Administrator of Pennsylvania, Supreme Court of Pennsylvania, Three Penn Center Plaza, Philadelphia, Pennsylvania 19102.
18.   Richard Morehead, "Briscoe, Labor Blamed," *Dallas Morning News,* August 1, 1974; Stewart Davis, "Proposed Constitutional Amendment Soundly Rejected by Voters," *Dallas Morning News,* November 6, 1975.
19.   Letter dated November 26, 1973, from Galen N. Willis, Deputy Administrator of the Courts, Supreme Court, State of Washington, Temple of Justice, Olympia, Washington 98504.
20.   Letter dated December 6, 1973, from William E. Lunney, Assistant Administrative Director of Courts, Supreme Court of Wisconsin, State Capitol Building, Madison, Wisconsin 53702.

21.  *State and Local Financing of the Courts (Tentative Report)*, op. cit., pp. 26-36.
22.  Letter dated November 19, 1973, from Jean Stabenoui, former Secretary to the Office of the State Court Administrator, Supreme Court Building, Carson City, Nevada 89701.
23.  Chief Justice Thomas Kavanagh, op. cit., p. 5.

## 3. THE EMERGENCE OF STATE COURT PERSONNEL ADMINISTRATION

1.  Roscoe Pound, "Principles and Outlines of a Modern Unified Court Organization," *Journal of the American Judicature Society* 23 (April 1940): 230.
2.  Edward C. Gallas, "The Profession of Court Management," *Judicature* 51 (April 1968): 334-36.
3.  *Establish Justice: Annual Report of the Circuit Court of Cook County* (Chicago: Circuit Court of Cook County, 1965), pp. 4-5.
4.  Friesen, Jr. et al. *Report on the Management of the Ventura County Courts*, 3 vols. (Denver, Colo.: The Institute for Court Management, 1972), 1: 5-6.
5.  "State Court Progress at a Glance," *Judicature* 56 (May 1973): 427.
6.  *California Unified Trial Court Feasibility Study* (San Francisco: Booz, Allen, and Hamilton, 1971), pp. 81-82.
7.  Colorado, *Constitution* (1876), art. 6 (1962), pp. 428-29.
8.  American Bar Association Commission on Standards of Judicial Administration, *Standards Relating to Court Organization* (Washington, D.C.: American Bar Association, 1973), pp. 75-76.
9.  List furnished by Richard F. Buckley, Research Assistant for the American Judicature Society, 1155 EaSt 60th Street, Chicago, Illinois 60637, with a letter dated October 17, 1973.
10.  "What's Wrong with the Courts: The Chief Justice Speaks Out," *U.S. News and World Report* 69 (August 24, 1970): 70; "Interview with Chief Justice Warren E. Burger," *U. S. News and World Report* 69 (December 14, 1970): 33.
11.  Letter dated November 19, 1973, from Donald Cullum, Assistant Court Administrator, Supreme Court of Nebraska, State Capitol, Lincoln, Nebraska 68509.
12.  Pennsylvania, *Constitution* (1968), art. 5, sec. 10.
13.  New Jersey, *Constitution* (1947), art. 6, secs. 6 (4) and 7 (1-3).
14.  Colorado, *Constitution* (1876), art. 6, (1962), sec. J (2-4); *The State of the Colorado Judiciary*, January 19, 1973 (Denver: Administrative Office of the Courts 1973), p. 1.
15.  Friesen, Jr. et al., op. cit., pp. 5-6; "Text of the Model State Judicial Article," *Journal of the American Judicature Society* 47 (June 1963): 12; *Justice in the States* (Washington, D.C.: Law Enforcement Assistance Administration, 1971), pp. 265-66; National Advisory Commission on Criminal Justice Standards and Goals, *Courts* (Washington, D.C.: U.S. Government Printing Office, 1973), p. 75; *A Study of the Louisiana Court System* (New York: The Institute of Judicial Administration, 1972), pp. 42-43; American Bar Association Commission on Standards of Judicial Administration, Standards Relating to Court Organization (Washington, D.C.: American Bar Association, 1973), p. 75.
16.  *. . . And Justice for All*, 3 vols. (Albany, N.Y.: Temporary Commission on the State Court System, 1973), 3: 29-30, 57; American Bar Association Commission on Standards of Judicial Administration, op. cit., pp. 79-80.
17.  State of California, Legislature, Assembly, Assembly Interim Committee on Judiciary, *Hearing on the Single Trial Court: A Plan for Court Reorganization in California* (Sacramento, Cal.: California Legislature, 1970), p. 30.
18.  *. . . And Justice for All*, op cit., 1: 45.
19.  *Study of the Louisiana Court System*, op. cit., p. 69.
20.  Pound, "Principles," op. cit., p. 230.

## 4. ANCILLARY DEVELOPMENTS

1.  "Organizational Concepts for a Unified Court System in the State of Michigan," draft (Detroit, Mich.: Ernst and Ernst, 1973), p. 24.
2.  Alan V. Sokolow, "The State of the Judiciary," in *The Book of the States, 1972-1973*, ed. Robert H. Weber, 19th ed. (Lexington, Ky.: The Council of State Governments, 1972).
3.  "Convention Comment," *Michigan Compiled Laws Annotated, Constitutional Articles 4 to End* (St. Paul, Minn.: West Publishing Company, 1967), art. 6, sec. 3, p. 278 (hereafter cited *M.C.L.A.*).
4.  The problem of civil delay in these courts still persists. See *Calendar Status Study—1964* (New York: The Institute of Judicial Administration, 1964), p. 4; *Calendar Status Study—1973* (New York: The Institute of Judicial Administration, 1973), p. 7.
5.  *M.C.L.A.*, 1: arts. 1-3.
6.  *M.C.L.A.*, 2: art. 6, sec. 3.
7.  Ibid.
8.  *M.C.L.A.*, 2: art. 6, sec. 4.
9.  Edward B. McConnell, "Court Administration," in *The Improvement of the Administration of Justice*, 5th ed. (Chicago: American Bar Association, Section on Judicial Administration, 1971), p. 13.
10.  *M.C.L.A.*, 2: art. 6, sec. 5.
11.  *M.C.L.A.*, 2: art. 6, sec. 7.
12.  *M.C.L.A.*, 35: secs. 600.225 and 600.8212.
13.  *M.C.L.A.*, 35: sec. 600.8212(4).
14.  *M.C.L.A.*, 2: art. 6, sec. 7.
15.  The Judges for the Third Judicial Court of Michigan *v.* County of Wayne and the Board of Supervisors of the County of Wayne, Board of Auditors of Wayne County, Treasurer of Wayne County (1968), as reprinted in *State and Local Financing of the Courts (Tentative Report)* (New York: The Institute of Judicial Administration, 1969), Appendix A, pp. 1-9; aff. 15 Mich. App. 713, 167 N.W. 2d 337 (1969); 383 Mich. 10, 172 N.W. 2d 436 (1970); aff. 386 Mich. 1, 190 N.W. 2d 228 (1971); certiorari denied 405 U.S. 923, 30 L. Ed. 2d 794, 92 S. Ct. 961 (1972).
16.  *M.C.L.A.*, 2: art. 6, sec. 1.
17.  Ibid.
18.  *M.C.L.A.*, 35: sec. 600.8101.
19.  Special Commission to Review Article VI, The Judicial Article of the Constitution of Michigan, *Report to the Michigan Legislature* (Lansing, Mich.: Michigan Legislature, 1972), pp. 4-5.
20.  *M.C.L.A.*, 2: art. 6, sec. 7.
21.  Special Commission to Review Article VI, op. cit., pp. 7-8.
22.  Norman A. Paelke, Jr., *1971 Court Personnel Study* (Detroit, Mich.: Michigan Supreme Court, 1971), pp. 3-4, 40-41.
23.  Fannie J. Klein and Ruth J. Witztum, *Judicial Administration—1972-1973* (New York: The Institute of Judicial Administration, 1973), p. 726.
24.  . . . *And Justice for All*, 3 vols. (Albany, N.Y.: Temporary Commission on the New York State Court System, 1973) 1:19.
25.  *Survey of Role Perceptions for Operational Criminal Justice Personnel: Data Summary, Project Star* (Washington, D.C.: Law Enforcement Assistance Administration, 1972), pp. iii-iv, 326, 368, 378.
26.  National Advisory Commission on Criminal Justice Standards and Goals, *Corrections* (Washington, D.C.: U.S. Government Printing Office, 1973), p. 313.
27.  Eugene H. Czajkoski, "Exposing the Quasi-Judicial Role of the Probation Officer," *Federal Probation* 37 (September 1973): 9-13.
28.  *The New Jersey Courts, Summary of Developments, Calendar Year 1972* (Trenton: Administrative Office of the Courts, 1973), p. 3.

29.   ... *And Justice for All*, 3 vols. (Albany, N.Y., 1973) 1:45.
30.   *Colorado Judicial System Personnel Rules* (Denver, Colo.: Colorado Supreme Court, 1970), Rules 2402, 2404, 2411-12, 2421, 2431-33.
31.   *Modernizing Louisiana's Courts of Limited Jurisdiction* (Chicago: American Judicature Society, 1973), pp. 141-42.
32.   *A District Court for New Hampshire* (New York: The Institute of Judicial Administration, 1973), p. 36.
33.   American Bar Association Commission on Standards of Judicial Administration, *Standards Relating to Court Organization* (Chicago: American Bar Association, 1973), p. 76; American Bar Association Project on Standards for Criminal Justice, *Probation* (New York: The Institute of Judicial Administration, 1970), pp. 91-92.
34.   James S. Campbell, Joseph R. Sahid, and David P. Stang, *Law and Order Reconsidered* (New York: Bantam Books, 1970), p. 555.
35.   *Justice in the States* (Washington, D.C.: U.S. Government Printing Office, 1972), p. 266. (Addresses and Papers of the National Conference on the Judiciary, March 11-14, 1971, Williamsburg, Virginia.)
36.   ... *And Justice* ..., op. cit. 1:45.
37.   *Citizens Study Committee on Judicial Organization* (Madison, Wis.: Citizens Study Committee on Judicial Organization, 1973), p. 99.
38.   National Commission on Law Observance and Enforcement, *Report on Prosecutions* (Washington, D.C.: U.S. Government Printing Office, 1931), pp. 159, 172, 181; National Commission on Law Observance and Enforcement, *Report on Penal Institutions, Probation and Parole* (Washington, D.C.: U.S. Government Printing Office, 1931), pp. 157-60.
39.   *Manual of Correctional Standards,* 3rd ed. (College Park, Md.: American Correctional Association, 1966), pp. 100-101, 103. See also "Organizational Concepts for a Unified Court System," op. cit., p. 332.
40.   National Advisory Commission on Criminal Justice Standards and Goals, op. cit., p. 313.
41.   The President's Commission on Law Enforcement and the Administration of Justice, *Task Force Report: Corrections* (Washington, D.C.: U. S. Government Printing Office, 1967), p. 35; The President's Commission on Law Enforcement and the Administration of Justice, *Task Force Report: The Courts* (Washington, D.C.: U.S. Government Printing Office, 1967), p. 32.
42.   National Advisory Commission, op. cit., p. 332.
43.   *Citizens Study Committee on Judicial Organization,* op. cit., p. 99.
44.   *A Proposal to Provide Management Consulting Services to the Michigan Supreme Court Systems Department* (Detroit, Mich.: Ernst and Ernst, 1973), p. 10.
45.   *M.C.L.A.,* 39: secs. 771.7, 771,10.
46.   Ibid., sec. 771.18.
47.   Ibid., sec. 771.7.
48.   Ibid., sec. 771.10.
49.   Ibid., sec. 771.12.
50.   *District Court Personnel To Be Transferred to State Payrolls* (Detroit, Mich.: Ernst and Ernst, 1973), p. 4.
51.   *District Court Personnel,* op. cit., pp. 2-3.
52.   *Recorder's Court Probation Manual 1973* (Detroit, Mich.: The Recorder's Court, 1973), pp. 2-3.
53.   *Annual Report for the Recorder's Court of the City of Detroit, Michigan, 1971* (Detroit, Mich.: The Recorder's Court, 1971), p. 2.
54.   National Advisory Commission, op. cit., p. 314.

## 5. CONCLUSION

1.   National Advisory Commission on Criminal Justice Standards and Goals, *Courts* (Washington, D.C.: U.S. Government Printing Office, 1973), pp. 1-2.

# INDEX

## SUBJECT INDEX

Advisory Commission on Intergovernmental
   Relations, 9, 32-33, 36
Alabama, 18, 37-39
Alaska, 33, 38-40
American Bar Association, 8-9, 13, 50-51,
   71, 79
American Correctional Association, 72
American Judicature Society, 2, 7, 9, 32,
   35, 45, 50
Arizona, 21, 33, 37, 49
Arkansas, 23, 38-41

Bethune-Jones, Inc., 2
Booz, Allen, and Hamilton, Inc., 19,
   34, 51

"Cafeteria approach" (or plan), 68
California, 14, 19-20, 34-35, 37-41, 44,
   49-51, 54, 56, 67, 69
Chief Justice's Task Force for Court
   Improvement (Texas), 20, 36
Circuit Court of Cook County, 45
Circuit Court of Wayne County, 74
Citizens Conference on Washington
   Courts, 22, 36
Citizens Study Committee on Judicial
   Organization (Wisconsin), 23, 36
Colorado, 6, 33, 37-41, 50, 57, 60, 67,
   71
Committee on Economic Develop-
   ment (New York City), 9, 32
Connecticut, 33, 37-41
Court administrator's offices, 2, 11, 48,
   52-53, 55, 60-61
Court of Common Pleas (Detroit), 21,
   62, 64
Court-related employees, 45-48
Court Studies Division (National
   Colleee of the State Judiciary, Reno,
   Nevada), 21
Court unification, 5-27, 77-80

Dade County (Florida), 19
Delaware, 15, 38-41
Duval County (Florida), 19

Ernst and Ernst, 3, 22, 35, 57, 59,
   65, 72

Fee offices, 8
Florida, 18-19; cities, 34, 37-41,
   45, 50

Georgia, 7, 23, 37-41
Governor's Commission on Judicial
   Reform (Oregon), 22
Governor's Judicial Council (Kentucky)
   34

Hawaii, 33, 38-41
"Hospital plan", 47

Idaho, 18, 38-41
Illinois, 8, 37, 41, 45, 49
Indiana, 17, 23, 37, 39-41
Institute for Court Management
   (Denver), The, 7, 32, 45, 50
Institute of Judicial Administration,
   The, 2, 21-22, 30, 32, 34-36, 38,
   45, 50, 67
Iowa, 6, 19, 39-41, 57

Joint Legislative Interim Committee on
   Elections and Constitutional
   Amendments (Kentucky), 34
Judicial Advisory Study Committee
   (Kansas), 34
Judicial centralization, 5-27, 77-80
Judicial expenses, categories of, 36-41
Judicial financing, 2, 28-42, 79-80
Judicial management, 1-2, 77-80
Judicial personnel, 28, 30, 43-69, 80
Justices of the Peace, 17-20, 22-23, 62

Kansas, 19, 21, 34, 38-41, 49
Kentucky, 7, 21, 26-27, 34, 37, 39-41,
   45, 49
Kentucky Bar Association, 34
Kentucky Citizens for Judicial
   Improvement, Inc., 21, 26, 34
Kentucky Crime Commission, 34

Law Enforcement Assistance
   Administration, 3, 65, 69
Los Angeles County Board of
   Supervisors, 34
Los Angeles County Superior Court, 53
Louisiana, 14, 20, 35, 37-41, 49, 71

Maine, 14, 33, 38-41
Maryland, 15-16, 33, 37-41, 45, 50, 57
Massachusetts, 35, 38-41
"Merit plan" of judicial selection, 13,
   45-46